Enterprise Modeling with UML

Designing Successful Software through Business Analysis

Chris Marshall

ADDISON–WESLEY

An Imprint of Addison Wesley Longman, Inc.

Reading, Massachusetts • Harlow, England • Menlo Park, California
Berkeley, California • Don Mills, Ontario • Sydney
Bonn • Amsterdam • Tokyo • Mexico City

EXECUTIVE EDITOR: J. Carter Shanklin
PROJECT EDITOR: Krysia Bebick
EDITORIAL ASSISTANT: Kristin Erickson
PRODUCTION MANAGER: John Fuller
COVER DESIGN: Simone R. Payment

Many of the designations used by manufacturers and sellers to distinguish their products are claimed as trademarks. Where those designations appear in this book, and Addison Wesley Longman Inc., was aware of a trademark claim, the designations have been printed with initial capital letters or in all capitals.

The author and publisher have taken care in the preparation of this book, but make no expressed or implied warranty of any kind and assume no responsibility for errors or omissions. No liability is assumed for incidental or consequential damages in connection with or arising out of the use of the information or programs contained herein.

The publisher offers discounts on this book when ordered in quantity for special sales. For more information, please contact:

AWL Direct Sales
Addison Wesley Longman, Inc.
One Jacob Way
Reading, Massachusetts 01867
(781) 944-3700

Visit AWL on the Web: www.awl.com/cseng/

Library of Congress Cataloging-in-Publication Data
Marshall, Chris, 1945-
   Enterprise modeling with UML : designing successful software through business analysis / Chris Marshall.
      p. cm.
   Includes bibliographical references.
   ISBN 0-201-43313-3
   1. Application software--Development.   2. UML (Computer sience)
3. Business enterprises--data processing.   I. Title.
QA76.76.A65M3452000
005.121--dc21   99-045160
Copyright © 2000 by Addison Wesley Longman, Inc.

ISBN 0-201-43313-3

Text printed on recycled paper

1 2 3 4 5 6 7 8 9 10—MA—0302010099
First printing, October 1999

En

wi

The Addison-Wesley Object Technology Series

Grady Booch, Ivar Jacobson, and James Rumbaugh, Series Editors

For more information check out the series web site [http://www.awl.com /cseng/otseries/] as well as the pages on each book [http://www.awl.com/cseng/I-S-B-N/] (I-S-B-N represents the actual ISBN, including dashes).

David Bellin and Susan Suchman Simone, *The CRC Card Book*, ISBN 0-201-89535-8

Robert V. Binder, *Testing Object-Oriented Systems: Models, Patterns, and Tools*, ISBN 0-201-80938-9

Bob Blakley, *CORBA Security: An Introduction to Safe Computing with Objects*, ISBN 0-201-32565-9

Grady Booch, *Object Solutions: Managing the Object-Oriented Project*, ISBN 0-8053-0594-7

Grady Booch, *Object-Oriented Analysis and Design with Applications, Second Edition*, ISBN 0-8053-5340-2

Grady Booch, James Rumbaugh, and Ivar Jacobson, *The Unified Modeling Language User Guide*, ISBN 0-201-57168-4

Don Box, *Essential COM*, ISBN 0-201-63446-5

Don Box, Keith Brown, Tim Ewald, and Chris Sells, *Effective COM: 50 Ways to Improve Your COM and MTS-based Applications*, ISBN 0-201-37968-6

Alistair Cockburn, *Surviving Object-Oriented Projects: A Manager's Guide*, ISBN 0-201-49834-0

Dave Collins, *Designing Object-Oriented User Interfaces*, ISBN 0-8053-5350-X

Jim Conallen, *Building Web Applications with UML*, ISBN 0-201-61577-0

Bruce Powel Douglass, *Doing Hard Time: Designing and Implementing Embedded Systems with UML*, ISBN 0-201-49837-5

Bruce Powel Douglass, *Real-Time UML, Second Edition: Developing Efficient Objects for Embedded Systems*, ISBN 0-201-65784-8

Desmond F. D'Souza and Alan Cameron Wills, *Objects, Components, and Frameworks with UML: The Catalysis Approach*, ISBN 0-201-31012-0

Martin Fowler, *Analysis Patterns: Reusable Object Models*, ISBN 0-201-89542-0

Martin Fowler, *Refactoring: Improving the Design of Existing Code*, ISBN 0-201-48567-2

Martin Fowler with Kendall Scott, *UML Distilled, Second Edition: Applying the Standard Object Modeling Language*, ISBN 0-201-65783-X

Peter Heinckiens, *Building Scalable Database Applications: Object-Oriented Design, Architectures, and Implementations*, ISBN 0-201-31013-9

Christine Hofmeister, Robert Nord, Soni Dilip, *Applied Software Architecture*, ISBN 0-201-32571-3

Ivar Jacobson, Grady Booch, and James Rumbaugh, *The Unified Software Development Process*, ISBN 0-201-57169-2

Ivar Jacobson, Magnus Christerson, Patrik Jonsson, and Gunnar Overgaard, *Object-Oriented Software Engineering: A Use Case Driven Approach*, ISBN 0-201-54435-0

Ivar Jacobson, Maria Ericsson, and Agneta Jacobson, *The Object Advantage: Business Process Reengineering with Object Technology*, ISBN 0-201-42289-1

Ivar Jacobson, Martin Griss, and Patrik Jonsson, *Software Reuse: Architecture, Process and Organization for Business Success*, ISBN 0-201-92476-5

David Jordan, *C++ Object Databases: Programming with the ODMG Standard*, ISBN 0-201-63488-0

Philippe Kruchten, *The Rational Unified Process: An Introduction*, ISBN 0-201-60459-0

Wilf LaLonde, *Discovering Smalltalk*, ISBN 0-8053-2720-7

Dean Leffingwell and Don Widrig, *Managing Software Requirements: A Unified Approach*, ISBN 0-201-61593-2

Chris Marshall, *Enterprise Modeling with UML: Designing Successful Software through Business Analysis*, ISBN 0-201-43313-3

Lockheed Martin Advanced Concepts Center and Rational Software Corporation, *Succeeding with the Booch and OMT Methods: A Practical Approach*, ISBN 0-8053-2279-5

Thomas Mowbray and William Ruh, *Inside CORBA: Distributed Object Standards and Applications*, ISBN 0-201-89540-4

Bernd Oestereich, *Developing Software with UML: Object-Oriented Analysis and Design in Practice*, ISBN 0-201-39826-5

Meiler Page-Jones, *Fundamentals of Object-Oriented Design in UML*, ISBN 0-201-69946-X

Ira Pohl, *Object-Oriented Programming Using C++, Second Edition*, ISBN 0-201-89550-1

Rob Pooley and Perdita Stevens, *Using UML: Software Engineering with Objects and Components*, ISBN 0-201-36067-5

Terry Quatrani, *Visual Modeling with Rational Rose 2000 and UML*, ISBN 0-201-69961-3

Brent E. Rector and Chris Sells, *ATL Internals*, ISBN 0-201-69589-8

Paul R. Reed, Jr., *Developing Applications with Visual Basic and UML*, ISBN 0-201-61579-7

Doug Rosenberg with Kendall Scott, *Use Case Driven Object Modeling with UML: A Practical Approach*, ISBN 0-201-43289-7

Walker Royce, *Software Project Management: A Unified Framework*, ISBN 0-201-30958-0

William Ruh, Thomas Herron, and Paul Klinker, *IIOP Complete: Middleware Interoperability and Distributed Object Standards*, ISBN 0-201-37925-2

James Rumbaugh, Ivar Jacobson, and Grady Booch, *The Unified Modeling Language Reference Manual*, ISBN 0-201-30998-X

Geri Schneider and Jason P. Winters, *Applying Use Cases: A Practical Guide*, ISBN 0-201-30981-5

Yen-Ping Shan and Ralph H. Earle, *Enterprise Computing with Objects: From Client/Server Environments to the Internet*, ISBN 0-201-32566-7

David N. Smith, *IBM Smalltalk: The Language*, ISBN 0-8053-0908-X

Daniel Tkach, Walter Fang, and Andrew So, *Visual Modeling Technique: Object Technology Using Visual Programming*, ISBN 0-8053-2574-3

Daniel Tkach and Richard Puttick, *Object Technology in Application Development, Second Edition*, ISBN 0-201-49833-2

Jos Warmer and Anneke Kleppe, *The Object Constraint Language: Precise Modeling with UML*, ISBN 0-201-37940-6

Contents

5.
Organization

Preface

Recent years have seen the convergence of many disciplines, facilitated by extraordinary social, political, economic, and technological change. Not least has been the convergence of business, information, and natural systems thinking into the new discipline of business engineering. This book describes how complex business systems may be designed and implemented using enterprise components and supporting tools. The CD-ROM at the back of the book contains implementations of the components and tools in Java and XML.

Business Engineering

The purpose of this book is to describe a specific way in which to model enterprises. The focus is on business rather than technological aspects, with examples describing large, complex, and adaptable systems. The book is intended primarily for practitioners of the emergent discipline of *business engineering*, and is of use both to business people who are sensitive to the strategic potential of technology, and to technologists who understand that business requirements must drive systems design and deployment.

Recent developments in computers and communications enable global business systems that are as much between as within organizations. There are no universal standards for such business systems, and such standards are unlikely to be established in the near future. However, concepts based on the principles of contract and law that have existed for thousands of years, and new insights from the study of complex adaptive systems, may be applied to disparate enterprise applications to enable them to work as though they were part of a single global business network. This book attempts to describe the main features of such systems.

The promise of software components has been recognized for many years, based mainly on the experience of other industries. Automobiles were handmade by craftsmen from raw materials until Henry Ford assembled cars using interchangeable parts, and electronic hardware was assembled by skilled technicians from discrete components until Robert Noyce developed the integrated circuit—but information systems must still be coded line by line by talented programmers. However, several key developments now make reusable software components not only viable, but essential to any enterprise that wants to survive into the twenty-first century.

- Ubiquitous networks connect almost every computer through standard communications protocols.

- The CORBA, COM+, and EJB component object models make interoperable software components feasible.

- Component design concepts, methods, and notations can be shared using the Unified Modeling Language (UML).

- Practical e-commerce standards and vocabularies using the Extensible Markup Language (XML) are under development.

- Enterprise modeling concepts are being developed and standardized in the ISO Reference Model for Open Distributed Processing (RM-ODP).

Each of these is necessary, but not individually sufficient, to enable widespread adoption of software components for enterprise systems. Together they provide the means to revolutionize the software industry to the same extent that the motor and electronics industries have been transformed.

An enterprise and its systems are too complex to understand from a single perspective, so its model is composed of several components, each representing a different area of concern. A component defines an aspect of the model in a specific frame of reference and at a particular level of abstraction, or from the point of view of an organization role. Each role defines a domain of expertise, terminology, and conventions that influence how a role player perceives the business world. For example, what is needed of a vehicle by a driver, an accountant, a transport manager, and a maintenance engineer differs according to their respective roles. In the past, this has caused organizations and their systems to be fragmented along functional lines, resulting in divergent purpose, discontinuous processes, and "stovepipe" applications. To prevent this from occurring, an architectural framework is required to link the components of the model into a coherent whole.

Structure of the Book

This book describes concepts primarily from the business viewpoint, and assumes that suitable software components can be created if a sufficiently precise business specification exists. The tools and components included in the CD-ROM attempt to illustrate the validity of this assumption. The UML notation and Java and XML languages are used in the design and implementation of these enterprise components.

Chapter 1 is an overview of the management and organization concepts that underpin the models that are described in subsequent chapters. Specific concepts of business purpose, process, entity, and organization are outlined to provide a context for the remainder of the book. The purpose of an organization is described in Chapter 2, with reference to strategy, planning, and contracts. It outlines relationships among data, information, knowledge, understanding, and decision making, which are also needed by an organization to learn and adapt, and to communicate its value to customers and other stakeholders.

Chapter 3 describes business processes as the means by which purpose is achieved. Process design, scheduling, enactment, tracking, improvement, and automation are covered. The concepts, tools, and components are suitable for formal process engineering and for the unstructured activities of ad hoc work. The human, mechanical, material, financial, intellectual, and other entities used and produced by processes are described in Chapter 4. Entities are modeled from various points of view to describe the different aspects of behavior required of them by processes.

Organization concepts are described in Chapter 5, with reference to their roles in adaptive systems, distributed networks, contexts for modeling, and so on. Organizations manage their processes and entities to achieve purpose, and work with others to form value networks. Certain ideas are presented to predict trends in e-commerce. The Appendix illustrates with simple examples how such concepts are used in real applications.

Conventions Used in the Book

Each chapter introduces its concepts with text and diagrams that are hopefully comprehensible to business people, without the need for detailed knowledge of technology. Object orientation is introduced through business objects—models that are not necessarily implemented in software—described and diagramed using the UML notation. In most cases, summary diagrams are used in preference to detailed diagrams to illustrate conceptual rather than detailed design. Words that appear in *italic* type when first used are defined in the Glossary.

The CD-ROM contains Java and XML implementations of the ideas and models described in the Appendix. Java code conventions are used where practical, but code is abbreviated, and many package statements, documentation, and comments are excluded in order to simplify the listings [Sun 1997]. No attempt is made to explore the business engineering process, or to describe business and software engineering artifacts and tools. However, the CD-ROM contains copies of a tool that enables round trip engineering of Java business objects using Rational Rose. It also includes detailed HTML documentation, and a tutorial to help readers acquaint themselves with its contents.

1

Introduction

The pace of change in the modern world requires that we find ways to manage the complexity of business systems while embracing the opportunities that are created by change—in particular technological change. Systems thinking provides a framework for sophisticated business models, and object technology is the means by which they are implemented across global networks.

Business Basics

Since time immemorial, human beings have produced goods and traded them for others in order to improve their quality of life. Over time, the introduction of money replaced barter with more sophisticated methods of pricing and accounting, which led to increasingly complex business processes. Recent times have seen the evolution of organizations for managing the large numbers of entities, particularly people, required to perform these processes. As we move into the twenty-first century, processes are as much between as within organizations, introducing yet another dimension of complexity.

Since time immemorial, human beings have produced goods and traded.

It is futile to attempt to understand all aspects of a modern business without some form of framework, or mental model, by which to manage its complexity. Every business has a *purpose*, usually to survive and profit, toward which its energy and enterprise are directed. The approach described in this book is that all aspects of a business flow from this simple idea, and are modeled by four related concepts—its purpose, processes, entities, and organization. These models may in turn be implemented in software using object technology.

Mental models help to manage complexity.

Business Strategy

Companies that create value for their customers will succeed.

Competitive pressure is forcing companies to rethink the ways in which they do business, and even the types of business that they do. The need for a coherent business *strategy* has never been greater, but the view into the future has never been less clear. No longer is it sufficient to define goals and plan and control activities to achieve them, because the goals, and the means by which they can be reached, change continuously. However, the company that focuses on creating *value* for its stakeholders is likely to succeed, and its strategy must be to identify and implement processes that maximize that value.

A business must differentiate itself from its competitors.

While this is necessary, it is not sufficient unless the business is able to differentiate itself from its competitors. An enterprise creates this difference by identifying its competitive advantage, and by maximizing the benefit of that advantage. By definition, this means that the company must do things differently than its competitors, which is not possible with standard procedures and packages. Indeed, "the ability to learn faster than your competitors may be the only sustainable competitive advantage" [Senge 1990]. To achieve this, a business must have flexible and adaptable systems.

Strategic hierarchy of purpose, processes, entities, and organization.

Successful enterprises develop strategies for defining and achieving their purpose. The purpose of an enterprise encompasses its vision, missions, goals, and *objectives*, which are achieved through its business *processes*. A business process requires *entities* such as materials, people, equipment, money, and technology, which the enterprise must acquire, develop, and organize. These relationships are illustrated by a strategic hierarchy (see Figure 1-1), in which the organization manages its entities, including technology, to perform business processes by which to achieve its purpose.

Figure 1-1   Strategic Hierarchy

Value Concept

The purpose of a commercial enterprise is usually to maximize the wealth of its shareholders. Other types of organization have different goals—the purpose of the military is the security of the state, nonprofit organizations have humanitarian objectives, religious orders seek to influence behavior, and so on. The value of each organization is determined by how well it achieves its purpose. Commercial value has two fundamental attributes: profit and risk. Profit is measurable using traditional accounting techniques, but risk is not often formally identified and quantified. It has been expressed qualitatively as profit, "now and into the future," and quantitatively by discounting future earnings by a factor related to the perceived risk.

Value has two fundamental attributes: profit and risk.

However, recent years have seen the emergence of new measures of corporate value, including the economic and market value added methods, the balanced scorecard approach, and value driver analysis. Formal disciplines of value analysis and value engineering, business process reengineering, statistical process control, and total quality management are used by companies wanting to improve their performance. Note that their primary focus is on improving the process by which the product or service is delivered, not on the product or service itself.

Focus on improved processes to deliver value.

"The difference between winning companies and losers is that winning companies know how to do their work better" [Hammer and Champy 1993].

Technology enables process improvement.

The electronic technology of computers, networks, databases, and other devices and systems that is now available to most organizations enables new ways of doing business. For example, the Internet allows a company to make and maintain contact with individual consumers, which leads to focused, one-on-one marketing processes. Design and implementation of such systems are far from trivial, however, and the risks of failure are high if the systems are used without a proper conceptual framework and methodology.

Business Environment

Global markets mean global competition.

Modern management needs not only to respond to changes in the business and technological environment but also to understand the risks and exploit the opportunities that result. Global communications and open trade policies have created global markets, which in turn lead to global supply and increasing competitive pressure. No longer can companies remain isolated and aloof from the rough and tumble of the world's marketplaces. To compete, companies have replaced traditional business methods and systems with powerful desktop applications connected by corporate databases and global networks.

Or have they?

Business needs must drive technology solutions.

The accelerating rate of change has left many companies bewildered and unable to deploy these technologies properly. A new framework for thinking, or paradigm shift, is needed to address these challenges now and into the future. Fortunately, a broad consensus is emerging in major companies around the world on how this can best be done. The brave new world of distributed business, which is driven by a desire for simplicity and the need for speed, understands that systems must be driven by the needs of the enterprise, not by technology. This requires that the business be modeled before attempting to implement its systems in software.

Mental Models

"Mental models are deeply ingrained assumptions, generalizations, or even pictures or images that influence how we understand the world and how we take action" [Senge 1990]. We all have mental models of the world, including models of the businesses at which we work and with which we deal. However, such models often are not shared by all the different stakeholders in a business, which may result in dysfunctional and provincial attitudes and behavior. It is essential to develop a shared mental model of the organization and its environment if we are to gain and benefit from new insights and to develop real consensus.

Shared mental models create new insights.

Mental models not only assist understanding of the world but also influence behavior toward it. They are, by definition, simplifications of reality, and tend to be biased toward the perspective of the person who developed the model. To build a shared vision, the assumptions underlying the models must be questioned and communicated to ensure that they are relevant and understood. A traditional authoritarian command and control organization is likely to have more difficulty in doing this than one having a culture of learning and change, because the learning organization continuously evaluates its environment so that it can adapt and improve.

Mental models also influence our behavior toward the world.

Learning Organization

A business, like any other organism, has a life cycle (see Figure 1-2). Successful enterprises learn to renew and regenerate themselves, whereas others just die. The life cycle of an organization starts with its founder's vision, which is translated into action through formal or informal business processes, with varied results. An effective organization learns from this experience to evolve its purpose, to

Successful enterprises learn to renew and regenerate themselves.

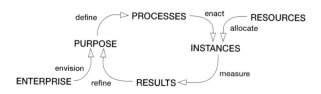

Figure 1-2 Business Life Cycle

refine its operations, and to improve its results. A learning organization is an enterprise that continuously adapts to challenges and opportunities in its environment.

The business cycle is at many levels within an organization.

Different business cycles occur at many levels within an organization. For example, long-term planning is typically conducted by senior management in broad financial terms for several years, budgeting is planned on an annual cycle, master scheduling may be done on a weekly basis, while shop floor activities are typically scheduled for cycles of 24 hours or less. The cycles influence each other in complex patterns of interaction, many of which are difficult to predict. Software tools, such as spreadsheets, systems dynamics models, and discrete event simulations, may be used to analyze these relationships and to help develop strategies.

Strategies are translated into action by processes and entities.

Strategies are translated into action through business processes. The entities used by a process are scheduled and allocated so as to maximize throughput at minimum cost. An inventory manager schedules receipts and issues to minimize inventory, a production manager allocates machine and labor capacity to maximize output, and so on. The ability to recognize and eliminate bottlenecks and other constraints is essential in most production and project environments [Goldratt 1992]. This requires information on which to base decisions.

Management exercises its imperative through decisions.

Management exercises its imperative through decisions. The quality of a decision is significantly affected by the accuracy, timeliness, relevance, and quantity of information available to the decision

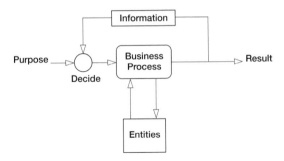

Figure 1-3 Adaptable Organization

maker. A proper understanding of the decisions, who is to make them, and under what circumstances they are to be made is essential. Some need immediate and precise data, while others use abstract and uncertain information gathered over a long time. Either way, the results of historical business processes may be used to adapt them to improve future results (see Figure 1-3).

Routine decisions are in many circumstances reduced to rules encoded into such business processes. Decisions that require knowledge and the power to reason can in some instances be automated using intelligent software. Systems that combine this kind of automated decision making with the intuitive abilities of humans can have a major impact on quality and productivity. The proportion of decisions made automatically increases as decision rules are progressively refined in the light of experience, emulating the adaptive behavior of natural systems.

Combine automated decision making and human intuition.

Enterprise Modeling

"The unhealthiness of our world today is in direct proportion to our inability to see it as a whole" [Senge 1990]. Systems thinking, the fifth discipline, is a framework to help manage the complexity of the world in terms of relationships rather than things. An understanding of the structures that underlie complex situations, and an

We need a holistic view of the world.

ability to see the whole as more than the sum of its parts, is central to systems thinking. In particular, it focuses on the emergent behavior of an organization, not just on the structure of its components. A business object model applies systems thinking to business concepts, seeking to describe economic activities, within and between companies and individuals, with simplicity and precision.

Notations

Technology means nothing unless it is directed toward the needs of the business.

In the past, much of the design effort in information systems has been focused on the technical aspects of database layout, process flow, user interface design, and so on. While important, this work is meaningless unless it is directed toward the needs of the business. Object technology has been used to simulate complex engineering systems for many decades, and has recently been applied to business systems. The Unified Modeling Language (UML) is used to illustrate how these concepts may be applied to enterprises, purposefully keeping diagrams very simple. Of particular importance are the organizational relationships between business concepts and things.

Relationships between objects are modeled by inheritance and associations.

Business is largely about relationships between entities, and UML class diagrams (see Figure 1-4) are suitable for static models designed to describe such relationships. An *inheritance* relationship shows how a class is extended to satisfy more specialized needs, indicated by a hollow-headed arrow pointing to the more general class. An *association* is a static relationship between instances of two classes, represented by a line between the classes. An association class extends an association to include attributes and behavior pertaining to the relationship. *Aggregation* describes how parts relate to the whole. A component may be owned by more than one aggregate at any time, its ownership can change over time, and it has an identity that is independent of its aggregate. An aggregate typically identifies its components by reference, indicated by an unfilled diamond.

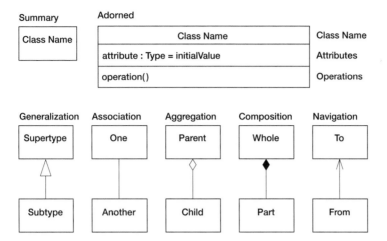

Figure 1-4   UML Notations

Composition is a stronger form of aggregation, which requires that a component be included in no more than one composite at a time, although its owner may change over time. A component typically does not have an independent identity, but must be referenced by means of its composite object. For example, the line items of an order are accessible only through the order to which they belong. A composite implies that some of its behavior is propagated to its components—for example, if the composite is copied or deleted, its components are also copied or deleted. Containment by value implies composition, so the attributes of an object, which are contained values, are instances of composition. Containment by value is indicated by a filled diamond.

A component need not have an independent identity.

Entities

The use of UML in this book is illustrated in the following sections by several different ways of modeling something—in this case a person. Things, whether physical or not, are called *entities* in subsequent sections and chapters. Entities are human, material, and financial resources, and other things consumed and produced by business processes. Entities internal to an enterprise include

A simple model is a class containing everything.

Figure 1-5   Person Class

employees, finance, equipment, inventory, technology, and know-how. Entities may also be external to the enterprise, such as suppliers, customers, contractors, and government and regulatory authorities.

In Figure 1-5, the basic object model of a person is a single class that contains the attributes and behavior that are needed to represent the person. While acceptable for a simple model, the approach tends to fail as it becomes more complex. Most business models are complex because different users have different requirements, and because the requirements change over time. A single unified or integrated description of an entity, although it is the goal of many modeling efforts, is typically large, inflexible, and brittle—the antithesis of what is needed by an adaptable organization.

Manage complexity by modeling the roles of an entity.

Complexity is managed by recognizing that a business entity plays a role with respect to each of its relationships with other entities. For example, as illustrated in Figure 1-6, a person might be seen by a company as an employee, by a retailer as a consumer, by a vehicle as a driver or passenger, and as a resource in the workplace. Each is

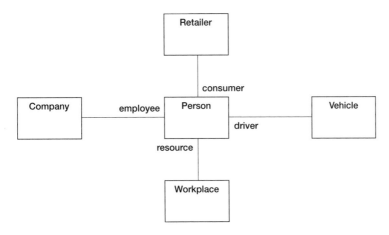

Figure 1-6   Entity Roles

a role that models one aspect of the person, relevant to a particular association. Convention states that if no name is specified for a role, it defaults to the lowercase name of the related entity; in this example, the role of `Person` would be `person` if the roles `employee`, `consumer`, `driver`, and `resource` had not been named.

Different kinds of things can play the same role, or have the same *type*, each of which specifies a package of behavior. For example, as shown in Figure 1-7, a company may be a consumer in its association with a retailer, and a vehicle might be a resource in the workplace. From the point of view of the retailer, both the person and the company are consumers, whereas in the workplace both the person and the vehicle are resources.

Different kinds of things can play the same role.

Because a business entity typically has many associations, it can have many types. This form of *multiple inheritance* may be illustrated in UML by Figure 1-8, in which an entity exhibits several kinds of behavior. While technically correct, this representation implies that the behavior of the entity is static, and that it holds in all contexts and at all times. This is clearly not the case in reality (whatever you choose that to mean), because the behavior of an entity depends

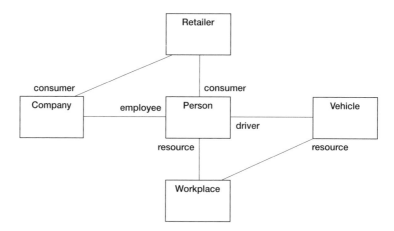

Figure 1-7   Shared Roles

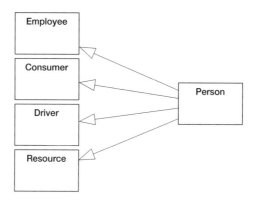

Figure 1-8   Multiple Inheritance

very much on its context and its life cycle. An alternative approach is to regard the entity as a composition of its *properties,* as illustrated in Figure 1-9.

Composite models help manage complexity.

The benefit of this approach is that behavior is separated into different aspects, which are of interest in particular contexts and at different times. This helps to manage complexity, because each is a partial model, typically involving a specific domain of knowledge

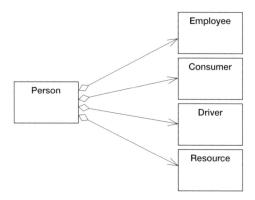

Figure 1-9   Entity Composition

and expertise. For example, an employment expert may know nothing of consumer behavior or resource management, but is never-
theless able to contribute to the model of a person as an employee.

This may be further refined to model applicants, recruits, trainees,   *Models may be pro-*
probationers, appointees, permanent and temporary situations, and   *gressively refined.*
retired, discharged, and deceased employees. Each is a body of
knowledge that is applied to an individual person according to the
life cycle of the person's employment. Each is an area of specialization that is specific to a particular domain, and is often of little or no
interest outside that domain. This, however, does not mean that
such properties apply only to one "kind" of entity.

Indeed, properties that model one kind of entity may be used in the   *A model of one kind*
model of another entity that has the same or similar fragments of   *of entity may be used*
behavior. Resource management, for example, is a specialized   *in the model of*
domain that is applicable to people, machines, natural resources,   *another entity.*
and other kinds of entities that have useful capacities. Similarly,
much of our knowledge of consumer behavior is applicable to both
companies and individuals, perhaps with some specialization. It is
clear that the properties of an entity change over time as it forms
and breaks associations with other entities. A person is a driver if

licensed to drive a vehicle, is a resource only when able to do work, and ceases to be an active employee on retirement. The approach proposed in this book is to model an entity as a composition of properties, each representing an aspect of its behavior.

An interface provides access to a component.

Finally, an entity may be modeled as a component that implements an interface to support each of its roles. An interface is a *stereotype* of class in UML, and is represented by the lollipop icon (see Figure 1-10). This is a convenient notation for describing enterprise components, which are typically business objects having predefined and reusable behavior. The notation becomes particularly useful when implementing systems using frameworks and commercial off-the-shelf (COTS) software components. Implementation detail is hidden behind the interfaces, enabling the designer to focus on the use of the component rather than on its implementation. It also allows different implementations, possibly from different suppliers, of components that provide the same behavior.

Actions

A business process defines how work is done to create value.

To be useful, a business model must describe not only entities and their associations but also how they interact. A business process is an essential part of a business model that defines how work is done to create value. As described above, an entity is modeled by its properties, and a process adds value by changing the state of one or

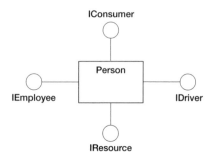

Figure 1-10 Entity Interfaces

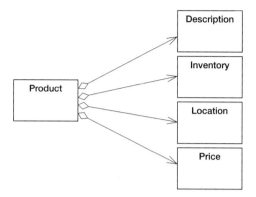

Figure 1-11   Product Properties

more of those properties. For example, as shown in Figure 1-11, a product might be modeled by its specification, inventory, location, and pricing. Each property describes the product from a particular point of view, specialized to a particular domain, and used by business processes that affect the product in a particular way. A product design team is interested in its specification, the production department plans and creates inventory of the product, shipping moves it to the desired location, and marketing prices it to maximize acceptance and profitability. Each adds value to the product (see Figure 1-12), albeit in a different way.

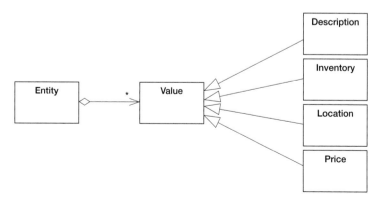

Figure 1-12   Entity Values

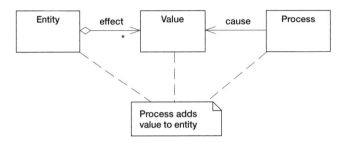

Figure 1-13 Process Adds Value

A process step affects one aspect of an entity.

This approach enables a general model of entities, processes, and value to be devised, rather than having to consider each instance separately. Because a particular process step is typically interested in only one aspect of an entity—the product specification is of interest to the design process; inventory is used and created by production, purchasing, and sales processes; location is changed by a shipping process—the business process can be partitioned in much the same way as the entity is partitioned. This is illustrated in Figure 1-13.

The same thing may have different names.

Each domain also tends to have its own jargon, and uses different terms and names for the same thing. The product may be a drawing in design, a stock-keeping unit in production, a (part of a) consignment to a shipper, and a product to sales. It has a name or identity—drawing number, SKU, UPC—for each domain or context in which it is used. An entity therefore may be not only described by its properties but also identified through them. This has significant dangers, because it fails to integrate the model into a coherent whole and may lead to isolated "stovepipe" systems (see Figure 1-14).

A process flows across domains.

Modern business requires processes that flow between such domains, both within and between organizations, so an individual entity in one <u>must</u> be the same as in another. Each entity is identified by a collection of names, each comprising a term and a context, some of which are unique [Kilov 1999]. A name is a kind of property used by business processes to identify an entity, and a role is a kind of

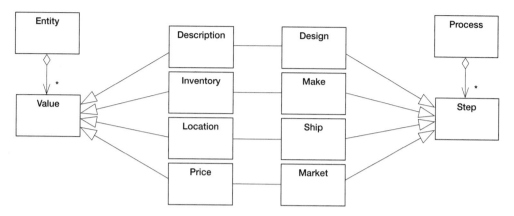

Figure 1-14   Entity Values and Process Steps

property that identifies the entity and defines the subset of its behavior available through that identity (see Figure 1-15).

Once an entity has been identified by a role, the role allows a process to use and change only those properties associated with the role. This argument will not enjoy universal appeal, but has proven to be an effective way to assemble complex and dynamic business entities from simple building blocks. It draws on the concept of a *facade* to assemble related properties as a single thing for a process to find and use, but allows each process step to act directly on its properties, thus combining the benefits of integration with those of efficiency [D'Souza and Wills 1999].

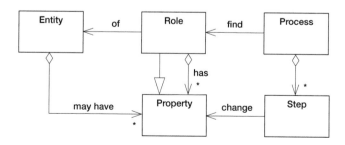

Figure 1-15   Property and Role

Plans

Future values are scheduled as objectives.

An enterprise does not merely react to current events, but also plans for the future. Planning takes many forms—financial budgeting, cash forecasting, inventory planning, production scheduling, and project management. Each form requires that the future values of its entities are scheduled, typically as objectives that are due by specific dates. Schedule dates may be ad hoc, but are often events or *deadlines* defined in a calendar. Deadlines coordinate separate processes, typically to manage resources of various kinds. For example, a set of supply processes may be scheduled to deliver components in time for a demand process in which they are used. Each satisfies an objective, which is to ensure sufficient inventory to meet the demands of scheduled sales, service, or production processes. While well established in manufacturing and construction, this approach is also applicable in other domains.

Schedule objectives, not actions.

A schedule is a list of objectives, normally in the sequence of their due dates or relative priorities. Note that objectives are scheduled, not the processes by which they are achieved. A financial budget, for example, specifies target values for each accounting period, but does not detail how the results are to be achieved. A production

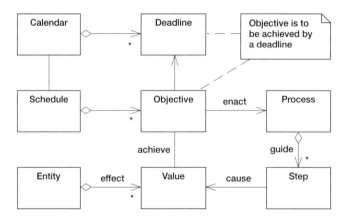

Figure 1-16   Schedule of Objectives

schedule similarly defines quantities of each product required, but does not directly schedule production processes. A process is enacted, or released, to achieve each objective according to the situation at the time of execution. For example, the duration of a process may vary according to workload, thus affecting when it must be started for an objective to be achieved by the due date.

Objectives do not stand in isolation, but are associated with other objectives, often in a hierarchy. Financial planning requires that budgeted costs be related to sales budgets to achieve gross profit targets. These are in turn related to expense budgets to ensure profitability. Purchasing and production schedules are similarly driven by demand forecasts and plans. An enterprise could not be coordinated if each business domain were to schedule its objectives independently of others. Coordination is typically achieved through schedules of higher-level objectives, goals, and missions, which together define its dynamic purpose.

Objectives support higher-level goals.

Rules

Often a business can define a standard response to a situation that occurs, or might occur, repeatedly. A business *rule* specifies the policy to be applied whenever the situation obtains. Simple examples are rules that specify replenishment of inventory when it falls below its reorder level, mailing of dunning letters to customers that fail to pay according to agreed terms, and sending e-mail to employees on their birthdays. Typically, however, the rules are more complex, and are recorded in contracts that specify the policies to be applied in all possible situations (see Figure 1-17).

Rules define the policies for particular situations.

When a situation covered by the rule occurs, an obligation is incurred to satisfy the rule. An obligation may be thought to be an objective triggered by the situation in terms of the rule. Rules are not just local to a business, but may also be defined by laws, conventions, standards, and contracts. A corporate accounting obligation is

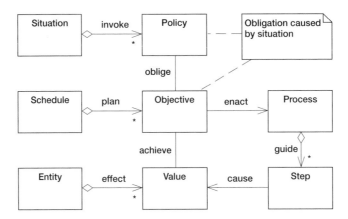

Figure 1-17   Business Rules

incurred each year in terms of tax law, certain routine maintenance objectives are required to satisfy safety standards, and payrolls must be met in terms of employment contracts.

Organizations

A party is a legal entity that contracts with others.

The final concept required to model our enterprise is that of a *party*, the legal entity that contracts with other parties, directs actors, and manages artifacts. As an *actor*, an entity is responsible for achieving objectives by performing the steps of business processes, typically according to the roles that it is able to play. Note that an entity may have more than one actor role, and so may be able to enact a wide range of process steps. An entity is affected by business processes through its *artifact* roles. An artifact that has useful capacity that may become unavailable because it is allocated or consumed is known as a *resource*.

Organizations manage entities to achieve purpose.

Business objects collaborate in a community, or *organization*, to achieve purpose. An organization, which may itself be an entity in a greater community, controls complexity by partitioning itself into manageable parts, and by coordinating the work between those parts. Each organization manages its processes and entities to achieve its own purpose, and collaborates with other organizations to achieve shared purpose. These concepts and relationships, which are used to build the enterprise models in this book, comprise the main elements of the *metamodel* illustrated in Figure 1-18.

The purpose of an organization describes its value to its shareholders, customers, suppliers, employees, and other stakeholders to define <u>why</u> it exists. Purpose includes the vision, missions, goals, and objectives of an enterprise, in which high-level vision and missions are abstract, of long duration, and difficult to quantify. These are supported by goals and objectives, which tend to be well defined, of short duration, and precisely measurable. This *hierarchy of purpose* links abstract vision to the concrete business processes by which it is achieved.

Purpose includes vision, missions, goals, and objectives.

Business processes define <u>how</u> work is to be done. They may be informal, conducted by people with little or no system support, they may be rigorously structured with a high degree of automation, or they may be anywhere in between. Business process engineering seeks to improve processes using formal modeling techniques and notations, and to identify <u>what</u> entities can be used to support the redesigned processes. Human users interact with business processes

Business processes define how to achieve purpose.

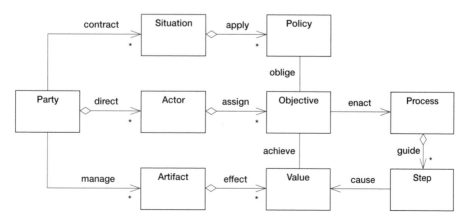

Figure 1-18   Enterprise Metamodel

by means of user interfaces and documents, which are now being supplanted by electronic messages that are handled automatically.

Purpose, process, entity, and organization are central to enterprise models.

The relationships among purpose, process, entity, and organization are central to the enterprise modeling concepts presented here. UML allows its notation to be extended through stereotypes, which group objects by their broad responsibilities, each of which may be identified by the keyword in guillemets (<<...>>) or by special icons [UML 1997]. In this book, enterprise models use stereotypes for the core concepts of purpose, process, entity, and organization, represented by the set of simple icons in Figure 1-19. While it may be argued that this introduces unneccessary "syntactic sugar," there are situations in which such icons help business people visualize the enterprise. Multiplicity indicators are also omitted from subsequent diagrams for simplicity.

An enterprise model describes a particular organization.

An enterprise *model* uses these concepts to describe a specific organization. For example, Figure 1-20 illustrates an organization that adds value by means of several manufacturing and distribution processes. The central purpose hierarchy, typically implemented by a financial ledger or a data warehouse, is used to set budgets and targets and to measure results. Data flows from business processes to the data warehouse and ledger objects, as indicated by the dashed arrows. In a distributed system, the processes are performed in

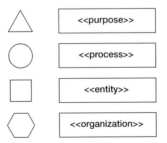

Figure 1-19 Enterprise Stereotypes

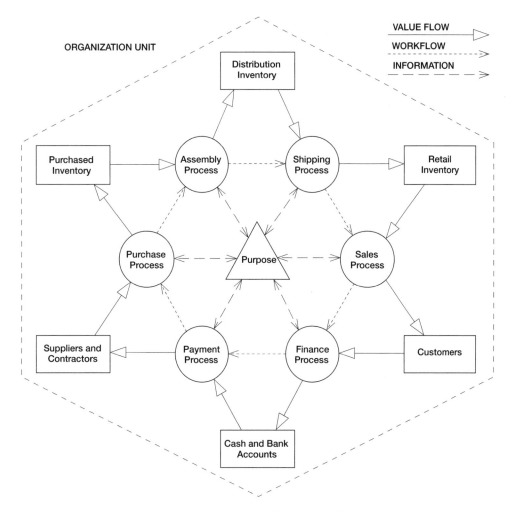

Figure 1-20 Centralized Enterprise Model

many locations while the ability to consolidate information in a
centralized data warehouse is retained.

The flow of control within and between processes is similarly modeled by workflow relationships, which are indicated by dotted
arrows. Workflow is an integral part of business processes, and does
not require separate design. The flow of value, or value chain,
between entities through processes is indicated by the solid arrows.

Workflow relates
process steps.

Business processes are thought to transform input resources to output resources with the intent of adding value and thereby profit. For example, a production process adds value by transforming materials into products, and a sales process adds value by exchanging inventory for cash or accounts receivable.

Value networks need sophisticated models.

While this model is adequate for small, centralized organizations, it is not sufficient for the radically decentralized business world that is now emerging. Traditional structures of ownership and authority are not reflected in the patterns of commerce and industry of today's *value network*. Instead, value is created and delivered through value chains that form and disband over time. Indeed, the day when such a chain is formed for a single transaction may not be far away. An extended mental model is required to understand these systems of distributed and largely autonomous units.

A value network is an open system.

Each hexagon represents an organization unit responsible for its own purpose, processes, and entities. However, instead of being thought of as a closed system with relatively little external interaction, it models an open system in which interactions <u>between</u> the units are as important as, or more important than, those <u>within</u> the units. The model has increasing relevance as the average size of organization decreases in response to information technology and falling transaction costs [Brynjolfsson et al. 1993], a unit in some cases being an individual. For example, companies that market goods or services over the Internet deal with individuals, and many services are provided by individual contractors or consultants. Even within large corporations, communication and coordination takes place among individuals and small groups.

The modern enterprise is a complex adaptive system.

Networks of largely autonomous units do not behave in the same way as organizations having central authority and structures of command. The behavior of insect and animal communities in nature indicates that the study of complex adaptive systems is more

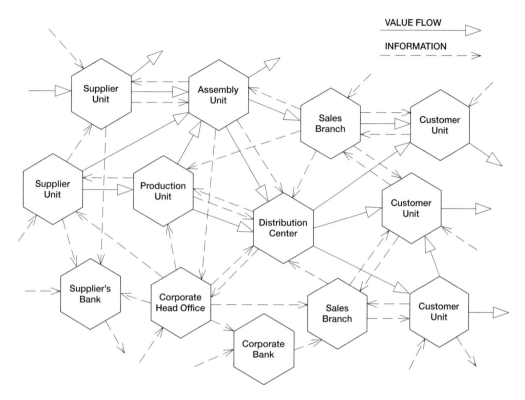

Figure 1-21 Typical Value Network

appropriate to an understanding of the distributed enterprise. How can independent, diverse, and loosely coupled organizations and individuals collaborate to deliver value? How can the exploding complexity of modern business be managed without centralized planning and control? How can everyone be party to the benefits of the new economy?

Summary

Businesses are too complex to understand and manage without mental models shared by their stakeholders. Such models must reflect the integrated, dynamic, and distributed nature of modern business, not the static organizational structures that characterized the past. Business objects create and communicate models of purpose, processes, entities, and organization—the building blocks of enterprise.

In a world in which political, economic, and technological barriers collapse, global business becomes the norm, and traditional strategies, practices, and systems fail. The study of complex adaptive systems helps us understand the new economic order, and suggests the kinds of business systems that will evolve as we enter the twenty-first century.

An enterprise metamodel is proposed to identify and describe concepts by which such business systems are modeled. The concepts are illustrated using UML to help business people communicate their ideas and needs to technologists. The remainder of the book elaborates, with examples, the description and specification of particular enterprise concepts. The Appendix indicates how information systems supporting such an enterprise may be implemented.

2

Purpose

The purpose of an organization defines why it exists in terms of the value that it can deliver. Purpose hierarchies relate relatively static strategic vision and tactical missions to dynamic operational goals and objectives. Measures of purpose quantify the goals and results of the business to enable planning and reporting. Centralized planning is being supplanted by networks of contracts to define purpose in distributed business systems.

Introduction to Purpose

Classical economic theory supposes that an organization has one or more goals toward which it drives in a rational manner. The strategy of an enterprise determines its long-term goals and defines the courses of action required to achieve them [Robbins 1990]. Strategy may be premeditated by means of a formal planning process, or may simply emerge as the result of significant decisions. An enterprise with more than one line of business typically has both a corporate strategy to decide in which sectors it should operate, and a set of business strategies to determine how best to compete within each sector.

The strategy of an enterprise determines its long-term goals.

Management theories and strategic styles evolve in response to changes in the environment, driven in particular by social, economic, and technological change. Strategic *planning* was fashionable in the 1970s, based on the belief that decades of stability and growth would continue indefinitely. The dramatic changes following the Vietnam War and the OPEC oil crisis popularized a visionary style of strategic management during the 1980s, championed by entrepreneurs with a vision of the future. The global competition and stagnant economies of the early 1990s had no quick fix, and so

Strategic thinking is influenced by the business environment.

led to the idea of the learning organization, able to constantly adapt to an ever-changing environment [Moncrieff and Smallwood 1997]. Since then, rapid technological change has offered great opportunities for agile enterprises, just as it has threatened those that have failed to evolve. Each of these developments has influenced the way in which organizations establish and monitor their purpose.

Purpose is without meaning unless it is translated into action.

An enterprise is a purposeful system designed to create value, typically expressed in an abstract, high-level vision statement, which is decomposed into increasingly concrete and detailed missions, goals, and achievable objectives. These relationships are illustrated in Figure 2-1 by an Ishikawa, or fishbone, cause-and-effect diagram [Schonberger 1982].

Abstract vision and concrete purpose are not obvious.

The understanding of cause and effect is an essential prerequisite for modeling the dynamics of an organization and its environment. For example, few are able to suggest how the return on equity (ROE) of a company might be improved, because there is no single process to create ROE. However, it is possible to calculate ROE from its input variables by dividing net profit by equity, as illustrated in

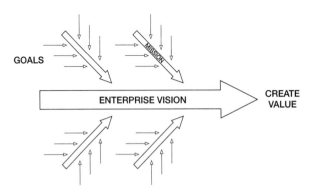

Figure 2-1 Purpose Fishbone

Figure 2-2. There is similarly no process for direct creation of net profit or for management of equity. However, they in turn can be calculated from their input values, gross profit, total expenses,

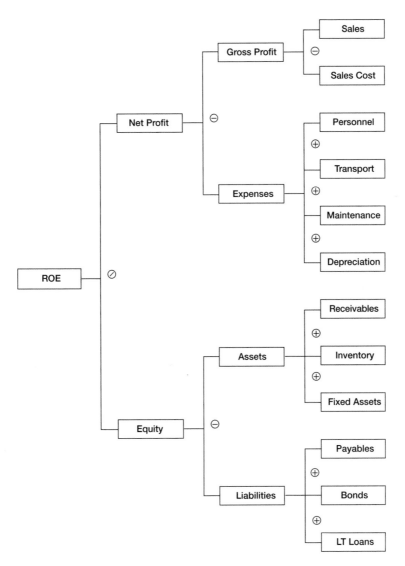

Figure 2-2   Value Driver Tree

assets, and liabilities. By recursively repeating this procedure, each input variable will ultimately be a value that is sufficiently discrete and precise to be planned, governed, and measured.

Hierarchy of Purpose

A value driver tree links purpose to processes.

Linking purpose at different levels is known as *value driver* analysis, and the resultant hierarchy is known as a value driver tree [Nickols 1997]. The value of a strategy is calculated by summarizing the tree values for its duration, discounted to present value at the target cost of capital, which is analogous to the *economic value added* (EVA) approach described below. Because it measures sustainable value, a value driver helps management focus on long-term shareholder wealth while understanding and quantifying the benefits to other stakeholders. The dilution of focus that results from multiple goals is eliminated by a driver tree having a single root—the vision of the enterprise. This multifaceted tree is a hierarchy of purpose.

The vision and mission are high-level purposes of an enterprise.

The hierarchy of purpose is the driver tree that relates strategy, tactics, and operations and provides a formal linkage among strategic, transactional, and analytic processes. Strategy defines the purpose of an enterprise, which at the highest level is its vision and the primary missions by which that purpose is to be achieved. Strategic purpose is abstract and difficult to quantify, has long-term consequences, and is of strategic importance to the enterprise. Subsidiary goals are the stepping-stones in this process, which are further broken down into specific and measurable objectives.

Shared purpose unifies the goals in an organization.

Without a unifying structure, there is no means of implementing the vision, and operations are likely to be fragmented and directionless. The nature of purpose differs among levels, depending on the following properties [Enterprise 1995]:

- Measurability: can one determine if the purpose is achieved?

- Time horizon: is the purpose achievable in the short or long term?

- Specificity: how detailed is the purpose?

- Relative priority: how desirable is the purpose?

Long-term purpose cannot be measured directly, but may be derived from the results of concrete, immediate, and measurable objectives. An objective is the planned value of an entity at a specific time in the future, and is modeled as a property of that entity.

Measures of Purpose

"What gets measured gets done" is an accurate if cynical observation of behavior in an organization—reflected in the elaborate budgeting and reporting systems found in most enterprises of any significant size. Information systems are also used to plan and control the progress of and expenditures on projects, to monitor the tempo of work in factories, to track the efficiency of transport systems, and in many other situations that need well-informed management decisions. Measures can lead, paradoxically, to less rather than more control, because management is able to monitor results without being directly involved in decision making.

What gets measured gets done.

Measures are not merely for management planning and control. Employees need measures to know how they are doing, as a basis for recognition of achievement, and to help identify problems before they become acute. Information reduces risk in decision making, and so is influenced by the decisions it supports. Operational decisions need concrete data for immediate use, while strategic decisions require summarized information to highlight long-term trends. Decision makers, whose data processing capacity is already nearing saturation, need information, not data.

Employees need measures to know how they are doing.

Decisions and Information

"If only I knew about it I could have done something about it." How often one hears this plaintive cry of a manager faced with an avoidable crisis. Information is the lifeblood of management because it is the key determinant of the quality of decisions. Risk is reduced by

Information is the lifeblood of management.

good information, which is accurate, timely, and appropriate. Information is therefore a resource that is used and produced by business processes. However, because it is used by humans, it has a number of special characteristics not found in other resources.

Information is needed to learn and change.

Information is also a valuable prerequisite for learning and change. The dynamic tension between where we are and where we want to be (see Learning Organization on page 5) requires information about both current status and intended purpose. A better understanding of a situation enables a person to creatively seek and find solutions to problems, and to adapt to change.

Information systems enable decentralization and autonomy.

Information systems enable decentralization and autonomy. Markets operate by exchanging price information with no other form of control. Management of an organization unit can be effected if there is sufficient supervisory information to indicate when intervention is required. In contemporary military organizations, "mission command and control relies on the use of mission tactics in which seniors assign missions and explain the underlying intent but leave subordinates as free as possible to choose the manner of accomplishment" [Sander 1997].

Information Hierarchy

The information hierarchy translates data into understanding.

The raw data from business transactions and other forms of data acquisition, such as stock market prices, plant condition, and so on, makes up the lowest level of information. Raw data is not yet processed, correlated, integrated, evaluated, or interpreted in any way, and so is of little use to humans. Information is data that has been processed so that people can use and understand it. Knowledge is information that has been analyzed and evaluated as to reliability, relevance, and importance and thus provides meaning and value.

Understanding is the goal of information systems.

Knowledge typically requires that information from many sources be integrated and interpreted to form a picture that transcends the information itself. For example, military intelligence is knowledge that transcends the individual items of information from which it is derived. Finally, understanding flows from this knowledge through deeper awareness and new insights. Understanding results when bodies of knowledge are combined to achieve a complete and meaningful mental model. It enables effect to be related to cause, thereby anticipating the consequences of decisions. The understanding of its users is the purpose of an information system.

An information system is intended to improve decision making by providing accurate information rapidly in a format designed to communicate its meaning. To design such a system properly, one must ask who makes the decisions, and provide appropriate information. A sales clerk needs to know the detailed credit status of a single customer immediately in order to accept an order, whereas the chief executive of a group of companies requires sales data to be

An information system improves decision making.

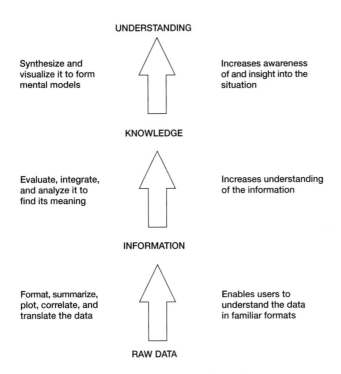

UNDERSTANDING

Synthesize and visualize it to form mental models

Increases awareness of and insight into the situation

KNOWLEDGE

Evaluate, integrate, and analyze it to find its meaning

Increases understanding of the information

INFORMATION

Format, summarize, plot, correlate, and translate the data

Enables users to understand the data in familiar formats

RAW DATA

Figure 2-3 Information Hierarchy

summarized from thousands of such transactions over an extended period of time.

A measure quantifies purpose.

Purpose is quantified, at all levels of detail, through measures that are individually suited to particular types of decision making. Key indicators measure strategic purpose, financial ratios measure risk and return, quality statistics measure conformance to specifications, and operational measures reflect the pulse of processes. Note that a purpose may have more than one measure, each being meaningful to a particular audience. A production manager measures throughput in units, a sales manager in revenues, and an accountant in profitability. Engineering, production, procurement, marketing, accounting, and other roles all subscribe to the purpose of the enterprise, but each has a set of measures suited to its own needs.

Decisions need accurate, timely, and relevant information.

The quality of a decision is significantly affected by the accuracy, timeliness, relevance, and quantity of information available to the decision maker. Management time is the resource that is consumed by information, so excessive or inappropriate information is extremely expensive and should be budgeted accordingly. This requires a proper understanding of the decisions to be made, who is to make them, when and under what circumstances they are to be made, and, most importantly, the knowledge on which they are to be based. Any data that does not directly support the decision is *noise,* which dilutes the impact of the relevant information and consumes management time in its interpretation. It is therefore critical to properly classify the decisions, the decision makers, and the requisite information and its presentation format and frequency. This is done by defining a minimum set of key measures by which to monitor the achievement of purpose.

Examples in Practice

A balanced scorecard has nonfinancial measures.

The *balanced scorecard,* as illustrated in Figure 2-4, is an example of a system that attempts to balance financial reporting with measures of customer satisfaction, process excellence, and organizational learning. Measures focus on the vision of the organization to

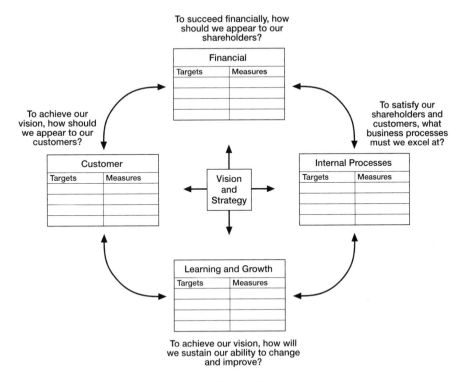

Figure 2-4   Balanced Scorecard

achieve a balance among customer expectations, internal performance, future growth, and shareholder value. The balanced scorecard is also used to help translate vision and strategy into action, and recognizes that management needs more than the financial information provided by most accounting systems [Kaplan and Norton 1992].

Stern suggests the single measure of economic value added (EVA) to capture the true value of an enterprise over time [Ehrbar 1998]. He proposes that incentive schemes for management should be based on EVA in order to align their decisions with shareholder wealth. Unlike the balanced scorecard, which has several divergent goals, EVA is a single measure of total factor productivity that is at the root of a hierarchy of all other measures. Saaty's analytic hierarchy

EVA and AHP use hierarchies to support decision making.

process is similarly a hierarchical framework in which the elements of a decision are defined, organized, and evaluated [Saaty 1990].

High-level measures derive from low-level transactions.

Decisions are supported by the few key measures of each purpose needed by a decision maker. Decisions at a low level can be made by direct observation of results, but at a higher level require information that has been collated from this data. High-level values are derived from lower-level transactions by means of sum, average, maximum, minimum, and more complex functions. For example, while it is impossible to measure sales of a product group within a region directly, it is quite feasible to summarize the information from individual invoices of products within the group to customers within the region.

A measurement hierarchy reflects a purpose hierarchy.

These relationships form one or more measurement hierarchies, which do not necessarily share the same structure as the purpose hierarchies but must be influenced by them if their information is to support the purpose of the organization. For example, a chart of accounts is a hierarchy of measures that calculates financial profitability, which is critical to a commercial enterprise, but which may not be central to a nonprofit organization. Construction, engineering, and other project-oriented enterprises require a different form of accounting, which is typically based on work breakdown structures rather than on conventional ledgers.

Purpose Components

Purpose components contract, schedule, and measure values.

Purpose components (see Figure 2-5) contract, schedule, and measure the values of an enterprise and its entities. Each must perform the basic function of establishing and quantifying purpose, and then must monitor results and feed them back to support decisions. The purpose hierarchy shown in Figure 2-6 is a generic component from which specific schemes are derived. Each purpose may have subsidiary purposes that form a hierarchy, a leaf purpose typically

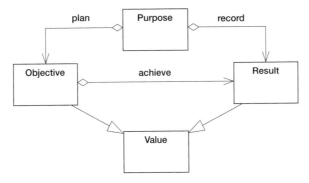

Figure 2-5   Purpose Component

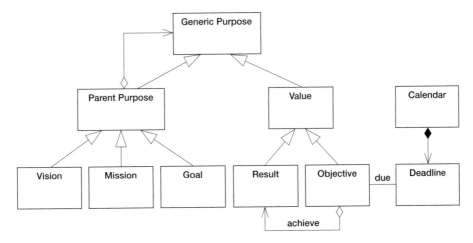

Figure 2-6   Purpose Hierarchy

being the value of an entity. An objective is a planned value that must be achieved by a deadline. The deadline may be a date, but is more typically an accounting period, scheduling cycle, or project baseline, each defined in some form of calendar. Results record the achievement (or nonachievement) of the objective. Note that several results may contribute to an objective, such as the values of invoices that are accumulated into sales during an accounting period. Values may be aggregated in different ways, the most common being to summarize a component's value into its parent in the purpose hierarchy. They may also be averaged, or be calculated by some other function in the parent purpose.

Financial Ledger

A ledger measures financial purpose.

For historical and statutory reasons, measures of monetary value are recorded and summarized in a financial ledger, which may be thought of as a specialized form of purpose hierarchy. A chart of accounts is a purpose hierarchy that defines how low-level posting accounts are rolled up into summary accounts. Each account has a set of accounting periods in which its budgeted value is planned and its actual value is recorded.

A chart of accounts is a purpose hierarchy.

A simple financial ledger is illustrated in Figure 2-7, comprising posting and summary accounts, budgeting options, and ledger and accounting periods. The future value of each account is periodically budgeted in order to predict profitability, cash flow, and other financial figures and ratios. Each account can calculate its budget values to facilitate the budgeting process. Summary accounts such as profit and cost of sales are calculated by adding the values of their subsidiary accounts. For example, the values of sales accounts are typically calculated from estimated sales volumes and prices, often by extrapolating sales history using statistical forecasting techniques. Costs of sales are in direct ratio to sales, usually based on historical experience. Expenses are estimated in a number of different ways depending on the type of expense and the mode of budgeting that is used.

Budget values are calculated in many ways.

The simplest method is to assume that existing costs will continue, perhaps modified to account for factors such as inflation, changes in efficiency, level of business activity, and so on. An alternative method is to calculate the costs of the required entities—the approach used for zero-based budgeting, in which history is not used as a basis for estimating costs. Other account values are typically derived by applying ratios to these values. For example, accounts receivable are estimated from the average number of days between invoicing

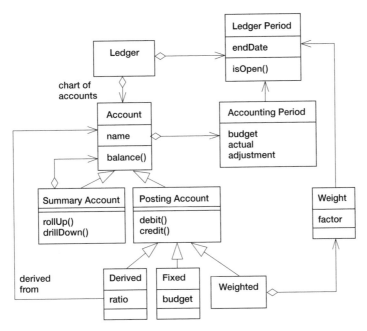

Figure 2-7 Financial Ledger

and payment, and inventory is calculated from the number of times
it is expected to be "turned over" each year.

A budget is not usually prepared for the year as a whole, but is divided
into monthly or quarterly periods so that interim results can be calculated and reported. An accounting period often does not coincide
with calendar dates. For example, it may always end on the last Fri-
day of the month, or on the twenty-fifth of each month. The number of working days, the seasonality of demand, the effect of weather
on expenses, and other factors might affect the relative importance
of an accounting period. These factors are taken into consideration
when calculating the period values of an account.

*Budget periods are
variable.*

The methods for setting budget values are overridden for each type
of account. A summary account merely summarizes the values of
its subsidiary accounts for each period. The fixed account sets each
period to the same value. The derived account multiplies the value

*Budgeting rules
are progressively
specialized.*

of the same period from the associated account by its ratio. The weighted account multiplies the budget amount by the weighting factor of each period. Other budgeting options are added by specializing the posting account in this way. Although these techniques are far removed from the reality of business operations, many organizations persist in using them to establish their purpose.

Aspects of an account are represented by segments.

A simple hierarchical ledger is suitable for a small company but is inadequate for an organization that has business units operating in multiple locations and multiple currencies, and that has diverse products and resources. Each of these aspects is codified into an account "segment" to represent a value and its qualifiers. For example, an accounting value may belong to a particular division, be allocated to a specific cost center or project, and be in a specific currency (see Figure 2-8). A collection of segments, one for each aspect, identifies the account to which each value is to be posted. In addition to aggregating values through the chart of accounts, each aspect may have a hierarchy, enabling values to be summarized by organization or project structure, location, resource category, and so on.

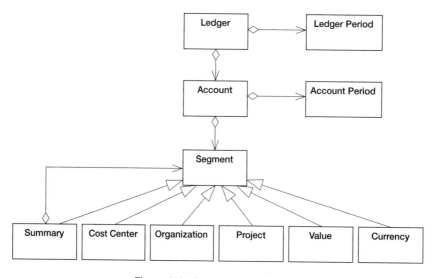

Figure 2-8 Segmented Accounts

Data Warehouse

Accounts record only financial value, and thus are insufficient for many of the operational and strategic information needs of an organization. Financial ledgers may be supplemented by more general *data warehouses*, which are well suited to the multidimensional nature of business purpose (see Figure 2-9). While a data warehouse is usually thought of as a technical artifact for managing large volumes of data, it may also be viewed as a business tool for supporting executive decision making—which is central to the purpose of an organization. Each independent aspect of the enterprise is represented by a dimension, or axis, of a data warehouse: a value axis records purpose; a process axis classifies activities by project or work center; another axis categorizes entities; the organization axis separates business units; and a time axis aggregates discrete periods. For example:

Information has multidimensional aspects.

- Value: sales, costs, profitability, assets, liabilities

- Process: fund, program, project, work center

- Organization: group, company, division, work group

- Time: cumulative, year, quarter, month, week, day, hour

Coordinates are classified into values, qualifiers, and the parent cooordinates of a summary hierarchy. A qualifier might define location in time or space, or specify another aspect of the enterprise. The time coordinate is typically determined by a calendar to identify the interval within which it occurs. Values may be aggregated up a hierarchy on each axis, reflecting the structural and other aspects of the enterprise. Executive information and decision support systems record and present information for management to understand and act on. They need to navigate rapidly from the summary information to more detailed data. The concept of drill down is well understood and is widely used by Web browsers and visual reporting tools. A data warehouse makes it possible for a user to navigate rapidly from a high to a low level along an axis using

Values may be aggregated up a hierarchy for each aspect.

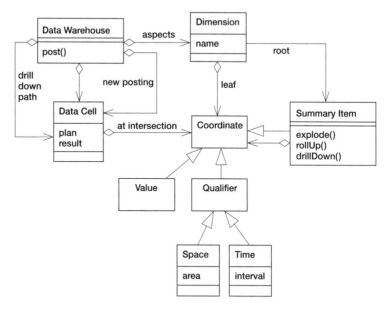

Figure 2-9 Data Warehouse

drill down techniques. The drill down freezes all axes except that being traversed, and the axis may be changed at any time. For example, the drill down path illustrated in Figure 2-10 results in "Sales in South Region for 3 January 1998."

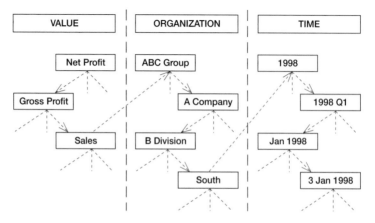

Figure 2-10 Drill Down

Work Breakdown Structure

The construction of large entities, such as buildings, engineering structures and facilities, ships, aircraft, and locomotives, requires planning and accounting more specialized than is available from a financial ledger. A *work breakdown structure* (WBS), as shown in Figure 2-11, is a hierarchy of purpose that defines the outputs or deliverables of such projects. A project deliverable, which is often complex and multifaceted, is progressively decomposed, or broken down, into its component items. At its lowest level, a WBS has measurable *milestones,* each to be achieved by a specific deadline. Each of these milestones is a kind of purpose by which the project is contracted, scheduled, and monitored.

A work breakdown structure is also a hierarchy of purpose.

Work breakdown items need not be physical entities, but must be things by which the value and progress of the project can be measured. Note that this is distinctly different from the approach by which process activities are grouped hierarchically into a process breakdown structure. The purpose hierarchy focuses on <u>what</u> is to be delivered, not on the processes that define <u>how</u> this is to be

Work breakdown items must be measurable.

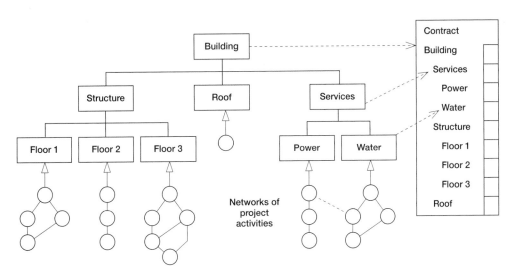

Figure 2-11 Work Breakdown Structure

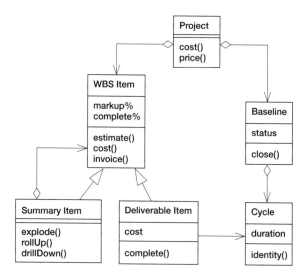

Figure 2-12 WBS Structure

done. This separation is particularly important when the work is specified by a different organization from that responsible for its delivery. A contract may be let against a specification without the contractor disclosing how the work is to be done, and with acceptance and payment depending on output delivered, not on the input time, effort, and cost.

A WBS defines the purpose of a project. A properly designed WBS therefore separates the purpose of a project from the activities by which it is to be executed, which in turn facilitates its contracting and measurement. It enables work to be partitioned, contracted, and coordinated between organization units with relative ease, often allowing them considerable individual autonomy and flexibility. Once a WBS has been created, however, it is difficult to change its structure, which limits its adaptability in dynamic situations. However, a WBS and supporting contracts are well suited to defining the purpose of the large, slowly changing projects that are typical of engineering and construction.

A contract to deliver such a project is typically made up of a number of line items, each of which references a set of one or more WBS items. Costs of WBS work items are calculated from those of their input resources and are rolled up into summary WBS items. These summary items are then used to estimate the cost of each line item, from which its price is determined. Line item prices are summarized into the contract price. Progress of work is estimated for each work item and is summarized into parent WBS items weighted by value. This is used to calculate the value of interim progress payments for invoicing purposes. Each contract line item therefore can have more than one invoice as the project progresses.

Contracts are composed of WBS items.

Purpose and Planning

Operational planning is required when financial budgeting and reporting are inadequate for decision making. While a business plan prepared by senior management to project returns and profitability can be expressed in purely financial terms, it is not suitable for planning the procurement, production, and sale of individual items.This is resolved by progressively exploding the business plan in a hierarchy of sales and production schedules and detailed capacity and inventory plans. Conversely, detailed operational results are rolled up to the business plan.

Resource planning goes beyond financial aspects.

The *master schedule* is "an authoritative statement of how many end items are to be produced and when" [Orlicky 1975], the critical link between aggregate financial and specific operational plans. The schedule is divided into planning cycles, each of which records the supply of, and demand for, a product during a cycle. A cycle is a batch or shift to which production is allocated: batches of specified quantity are typical of discrete manufacture, whereas shifts of particular duration are typical of process and flow production.

A master schedule lists demand for and supply of products.

Firm demand for a product is calculated by summarizing sales and production requirements for each cycle to the demand horizon,

Demand is forecast to the forecast horizon.

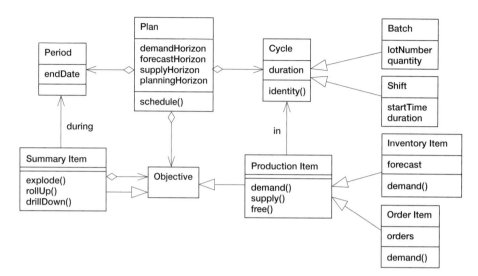

Figure 2-13   Production Planning

which is normally expressed as a number of cycles. Demand of make-to-inventory products may be forecast for an additional number of cycles. Firm demand replaces, or consumes, the forecast demand. Supply processes, which include purchase, manufacturing, and distribution orders, are scheduled to satisfy this demand. Supplies of make-to-inventory products may be planned for more periods than are scheduled. Firm and forecast demand cycles are called, respectively, the demand and forecast horizons, and scheduled and planned supply, the scheduling and planning horizons (see Capacity on page 121).

Supply is suggested to meet demand.

The surplus, or free quantity, of supply over demand of make-to-stock products is "available to promise" to new demand processes. The earliest date on which capacity is available for make-to-order products is "available to book" to demand processes. The master schedule suggests supply quantities and dates to meet the firm and forecast demand of each product, taking into account its inventory and order policies. The master schedule *releases* processes to supply these quantities for periods that are within the schedule horizon.

Note that these processes may be created by one organization unit but executed by another unit, allowing the master schedule to coordinate work between units.

This type of hierarchical planning optimizes resource usage at the price of reduced flexibility and adaptability. By launching orders weeks or months in advance of requirements, production schedules are effectively frozen. Some flexibility can be gained by carrying surplus inventories, by rationalizing components and assemblies, and by deferring final assembly and configuration. Although a master schedule is an appropriate tool for planning the purpose of some enterprises, agile organizations require more flexible and responsive ways in which to coordinate their activities.

Hierarchical systems optimize the use of resources.

Purpose and Policy

Many situations that do or might happen regularly in business can be handled by establishing policies that define the actions to be taken when they occur. A *policy* is defined as a set of rules related to a particular *situation*, and a rule may be an obligation or an authorization, which is either a permisson or a prohibition. An obligation is activated by conditions that make it active and has conditions that indicate when it is fulfilled, cancelled, or violated. The purpose of the example in Figure 2-14 is to manage inventory by applying two policies—one when inventory is low, and the other when it is high.

Situations that occur regularly are handled by policies.

Should the inventory balance be below the minimum, it is replenished. If it is above the maximum, it is reduced by selling at a discount; however, if this is not possible for any reason, the surplus may be written off. Whenever inventory is below the minimum or above the maximum, the rule creates an appropriate objective by which it is (to be) satisfied. The policy therefore eliminates the need for explicit planning of such inventory transactions, thus simplifying their management.

A policy eliminates the need for explicit planning.

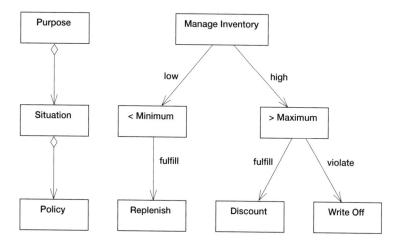

Figure 2-14   **Manage Inventory**

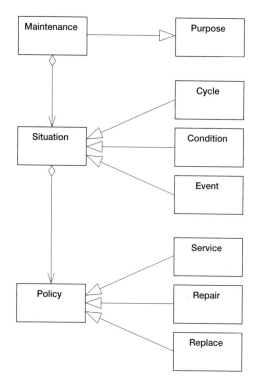

Figure 2-15   **Maintenance Policy**

The purpose of planned maintenance is typically to ensure the *Policies have purpose.* availability of a maintained item at acceptable cost. The situations under which maintenance is required might be specified in relation to a time or usage cycle (such as every three months, or at ten thousand miles), a condition (for example, when oil pressure drops below a minimum value), or an event (such as during annual shut-down). The policies to be applied in these situations range from simple inspection, lubrication, or service to complete replacement of the item or its components (see Figure 2-15).

Purpose and Contract

These concepts can be extended to contracts, illustrated in Figure 2-16. *A contract is a state-* Contracts are statements of intent that regulate behavior among *ment of purpose.* organizations and individuals, ranging from international trade law

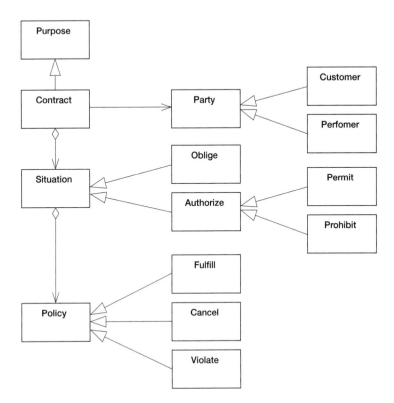

Figure 2-16 Generic Contract

to verbal offer and acceptance between people. A contract is instantiated as a set of obligations between its parties which are fulfilled, canceled, or violated. A good contract defines the rights and obligations in every possible case, including cancellation and violation. A contract is therefore a statement of purpose that defines the expected performance, lead times and deadlines, period of validity, and other conditions that satisfy obligations incurred in terms of its clauses.

A party cannot simply instruct another party to perform.

One party cannot simply instruct another party to perform, because each is an autonomous entity, with no power relationship between them [Verharen 1997]. They must first come to an agreement about, and record in a contract, the terms and conditions under which the service is to be performed. A contract defines the permissions, prohibitions, and obligations that apply to interactions between the parties, including the policies that govern violations of the contract. Obligations that have been incurred but not yet fulfilled are typically scheduled as objectives in much the same way as in planning. Standard scheduling techniques determine if sufficient resources are available to satisfy the obligation. If not, the party in turn may incur *upstream* obligations or may choose to violate the contract.

Outsourcing converts rules into contracts.

The maintenance policy described above may be extended into the maintenance contract in Figure 2-17 by specifying the parties to the contract and (optionally) the items to be maintained. The main difference is that the performer does the maintenance on behalf of the customer under the terms and conditions set out in the contract. Indeed, often there is no change except in the legal basis on which the work is done, as exemplified by the "outsourcing" of such functions by many organizations.

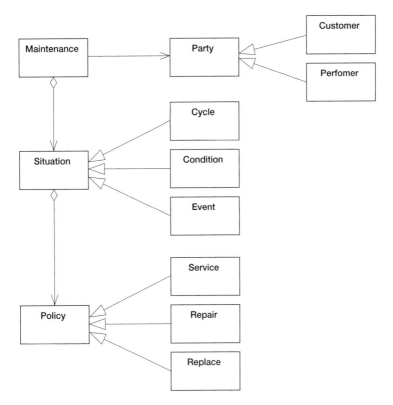

Figure 2-17   Maintenance Contract

Summary

The juxtaposition of ideas in this chapter reflects the ad hoc way in which most organizations establish and monitor their purpose. The link between corporate strategy and operational activities is often tenuous, and is usually expressed in monetary terms through financial ledgers. Budgeting is often the means by which purpose is planned, and financial reporting the primary means by which it is measured.

Many organizations recognize the need for improved planning and control. The work breakdown structure in project environments is an example of a purpose hierarchy that combines operational and financial elements. Maintenance systems often have no financial aspects but instead use statistical techniques to analyze reliability and availability. ERP systems have comprehensive hierarchical schedules for planning and controlling the purpose of the enterprise.

Modern business is frequently too complex for such centralized planning and control, and thus increasingly relies on contracts to establish and regulate purpose within and between organizations. Parties to such agreements operate autonomously without centralized control, coordinating their activities by incurring and fulfilling obligations in terms of contracts. While traditionally the domain of lawyers, contracts may be formalized into machine-readable documents for automating much of the behavior of organizations.

3

Processes

A business process defines how an organization achieves its purpose, and is designed to add value. It is composed of atomic process steps at the lowest level, which are related to each other by workflow rules. A process step is assigned to an organization role to enable workflow and security management. A user interface or document enables a human actor having the role to interact with the process.

What Is a Business Process?

A business process defines how an organization achieves its purpose. Strategic processes develop vision and missions, and tactical and operational processes are designed to achieve specific goals and objectives. The term "business process" has many definitions because a process impacts all aspects of an organization. Selected definitions are as follows.

A business process defines how business purpose is to be achieved.

- Concise Oxford Dictionary: A process is a course of action, a series of operations, or a series of changes.

- Object Management Group: Processes represent the flow of work and information throughout the business. These processes act on the business entities to cause the business to function. Business processes may be long-lived, such as an order life cycle, or may be short-lived, such as an end-of-year report. Long-life-cycle business processes are typically part of business process reengineering (BPR) analysis [OMG 1995].

- ISO 9000: Every organization exists to accomplish value-adding work. The work is accomplished through a network of processes. Every process has inputs, and the outputs are the results

Every organization exists to add value.

of the process. The structure of the network is not usually a simple sequential structure, but typically is quite complex [ISO 9000-1 1994].

- Ivar Jacobson: A business process is the set of internal activities performed to serve a customer. The purpose of each business process is to offer each customer the right product or service, with a high degree of performance measured against cost, longevity, service and quality [Jacobson et al. 1995].

- Peter Senge: A process is a circle of causality that describes a feedback loop of cause and effect. From the systems perspective, the human actor is part of the feedback process, not standing apart from it [Senge 1990].

- CMU Software Engineering Institute: A set of partially ordered steps intended to reach a goal. A process is decomposable into process steps and process components. The former represent the smallest, atomic level; the latter may range from individual process steps to very large parts of processes [CMU/SEI-93-TR-23].

Such definitions are used to model, design, and implement business processes, which can range from simple, linear process steps to complex networks of interdependent activities. The purpose objects described in Chapter 2 create needs and incur obligations which are satisfied and fulfilled by processes described in this chapter.

Process Steps

Continuous processes are modeled by discrete events.

Stuff happens continuously, but we choose to model it as a series of discrete *events*. Social and other contracts have long recognized this fact in the concept of a legal event or transaction, typically to record some exchange of value. The event is, however, an artificial concept designed to help model the progress of the process by which the value is exchanged. As a device by which to manage complexity, it is widely understood and applied. To use a really weird example, the gargantuan natural process that occurred when Mount St.

Helens erupted is regarded as a geographic event to those interested in its long-term effects.

A process step is the basic building block of a business process, representing a single *unit of work,* which is not divided into smaller steps. A process step, also known as an activity or a transaction, is executed either in full or not at all. Being atomic, a process step uniquely identifies a business event, and may be used for auditing and other purposes. For example, the sum of values posted by the process step to a financial ledger must be zero if the ledger is to remain in balance. Before it can be executed, a process step checks this fact, and raises an exception if the balance is not zero. Business rules may be enforced by checking conditions before, and by verifying conditions after a process step is completed.

An atomic step is the basic building block of a business process.

Human actors are an integral part of any process that is not entirely automated, and each process step has a *user interface* by which it is viewed and controlled by the actor. The user interface enables an actor to enter and modify attributes and to start, suspend, restore, cancel, or complete the process step. Each step typically also has an electronic or paper *document* for users who do not have direct access to the process. For example, a sales invoice process step typically creates an equivalent sales invoice document for the customer. Each step records a business event in an audit trail, transaction log, or other history of business activity.

Human actors are an integral part of a process.

Finally, a process step may access and change the state of one or more business entities and post information to a financial ledger or data warehouse. A sales invoice verifies the credit status of the customer, debits the sale amount to its receivable account, and credits the appropriate sales and tax accounts. Should it be an inventory sale, the inventory balance of each line item is reduced by the quantity sold, and the cost of sales account is debited with its cost. The actions within a process step vary considerably among different

A process step can change the states of other objects.

processes, companies, and domains, and thus tend to be customized in most situations.

Compound Processes

Compound processes are too complex for a single step.

Many business processes are too complex to be done in a single step, and therefore must be accomplished by a sequence of steps. A purchase process, for example, might have separate steps for requesting, authorizing, ordering, receiving, inspecting, and paying. Each step might be performed by a different person, at a different time, in a different location. However, they are all part of the same process and must be executed in a proper sequence by people having appropriate ability and authority. A *compound process* is composed of a set of process steps, with *workflow* rules to specify their sequential and other dependencies.

A business process is intended to achieve some purpose.

The steps of a business process have a variety of dependencies, including the simple precedence of project networks, the *split* and *join* of workflow systems, and other relationships that depend on the current states of the process and its associated entities. Figure 3-1

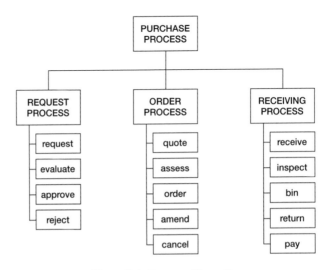

Figure 3-1 Process Hierarchy

illustrates how a complex process may be hierarchically decomposed. Process definitions of this type are used in production and project work, in which each step must occur in sequence and be done in a specific way. They are not well suited to knowledge workers, who require autonomy and flexibility in their work, preferring *ad hoc processes* that they can adapt to their needs.

Process Definition

The Center for Coordination Science at MIT aims to compile a *process handbook* detailing best work practices at a variety of different companies [Malone et al. 1997]. Business processes would be classified in the handbook along several dimensions, as shown in Figure 3-2. Sales might be classified by how they are done into categories of direct sales, retail, mail-order sales, and Internet sales. Alternatively, they might be grouped by what is sold into categories of products and services. Malone proposes a trade-off matrix between alternatives on each dimension to enable process options to be evaluated.

The process handbook would classify business processes.

A process step is progressively specialized by inheriting from a more general process class, which allows each to be refined to satisfy precise requirements. However, type inheritance cannot be applied to

Specialization restricts process combinations.

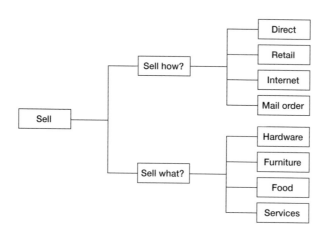

Figure 3-2 Process Specialization

a compound process as a whole, because specialization in this case limits process behavior. The most general process may have its component steps and workflow in any combination, and is specialized by progressively removing options. For example, a general purchase process allows many different sequences of inquiry, quotation, order, delivery, and payment. However, a specific process is restricted to one or a few of these combinations. Specialization therefore restricts rather than extends process behavior.

Business processes can be categorized.

The informal taxonomy shown in Figure 3-3 groups processes into broad categories that have similar behavior. An exchange process acquires one entity in exchange for another, such as the sale of a product for cash. A production process consumes input resources in order to transform them into goods or services. Financial processes manage cash and other financial instruments according to specialized monetary behavior and accounting rules. Designs, specifications,

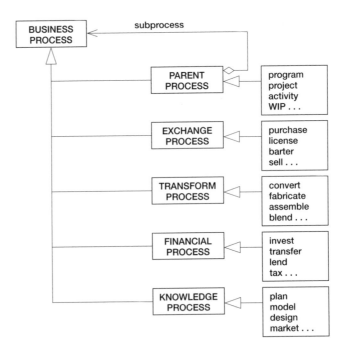

Figure 3-3 Process Taxonomy

procedures, and other intellectual capital are created and maintained by knowledge processes. Other classification schemes may be equally valid, because processes are as diverse as the businesses in which they are conducted. All business processes, however, are examples of the fundamental *workflow loop*, by which needs are communicated and satisfied.

Workflow Loop

"The molecular element of all business processes is the workflow loop, an interaction between two people in which one—the performer—fulfills a commitment to the satisfaction of the other—the customer" [White and Fischer 1994]. This concept is illustrated by the role activity diagram in Figure 3-4. A role activity diagram relates steps in a process to the organization roles that are responsible for their execution [Ould 1995]. A role may have several instances, each of which is a position or post in the organization. Every post potentially has an incumbent, which is the person who is assigned to the position. A role can be played by more than one person, and a person can play more than one role. Roles may also be performed by nonhuman actors.

The workflow loop is the basis of all business processes.

A customer may be a performer for another customer in a chain of workflow loops to satisfy complex needs. A process definition specifies the preferred way for work to be done, without imposing

A network of workflow loops is a business process.

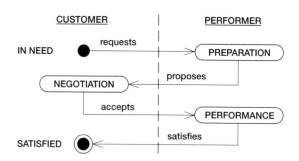

Figure 3-4 Workflow Loop

unnecessary constraints on users. Business process reengineering and total quality management techniques are typically used to improve processes, and are often done concurrently with formal process definition. For example, a well-designed process might minimize the number of "hand-offs" between people to reduce cycle time and eliminate split responsibilities [Hammer and Champy 1993]. In turn, this reduces the number of roles and potentially the number of steps in the process.

Processes are designed to prevent rather than correct errors.

Processes are designed to prevent rather than correct defects, identifying and eliminating errors at the source, thus eliminating *non-value-adding* operations. The cycle times of processes are minimized by reducing or eliminating setups, transfers, queuing, rework, or batching, and by working concurrently rather than sequentially. When feasible, work is automatically forwarded to the next step, and is highlighted for attention when forwarding is not feasible. Process-relevant data is captured once at the source, and is thereafter stored and distributed, typically using database and network technologies.

A scenario shows the flow of work through a business process.

A *scenario* shows the flow of work through a business process, which may be sequential with branching points, parallel with rendezvous points, or executed in an ad hoc sequence controlled by the user [White and Fischer 1994]. A scenario is a process instance that illustrates a specific set of steps that may occur. Combining all possible scenarios, the business process can be fully defined. Many production, engineering, and office processes are formally defined in this way, but others are left to the discretion of users.

Value chains are implemented by processes.

Processes do not stand in isolation, but are combined to form chains to deliver value to their ultimate customers. Enterprise resource planning systems integrate sales, manufacturing, and procurement plans and processes to deliver goods and services to their customers. Supply chain management focuses on transportation logistics to move components from supply centers to demand locations. Modern enterprises require integration of all aspects of their systems, from transactions to decision support, between strategy and operations, and across organizational boundaries [OMG 1997]. Coordination of such systems is extremely complex and is beyond the capability of traditional command and control systems—even in the military, where authority is absolute [Sander 1997].

The granularity with which a process is modeled is not necessarily the same for all purposes. For example, production processes may be created in detail for scheduling, but may only need a few major transactions for costing and accounting purposes. Other measures can be added to a process with ease. The variability of value added indicates the risk of a process, its cycle time is a measure of responsiveness, the ratio between its actual and standard duration is a measure of efficiency, and so on.

Process granularity varies among different purposes.

Process Monitoring

A process is designed to achieve a purpose, each of which may have a number of measures for planning and tracking its progress. These measures can be updated automatically by the process, and an essential aspect of process design is the definition of when and how this information is to be posted to financial ledgers and data warehouses. Some measures apply to all kinds of processes, and thus can be implemented by a generic process class, including:

Measurement is an essential part of process design.

- Productivity: output value as a percentage of input cost

- Value added: output value less input cost

- Cycle time: start date/time to finish date/time

- Queue length: average length of work item queue

- Quality index: number of defects as a percentage of process instances

Generic measures apply to all processes.

Such measures form an excellent basis for global performance norms, work standards, and variance reporting. They also quantify the benefits of process improvement and adaptation.

"The primary threats to our survival, both of our organizations and of our societies, come not from sudden events but from slow, gradual processes" [Senge 1990].

Process measures highlight trends.

Without proper measurement, it is almost impossible to detect such trends in an organization. Long-term tracking of relative trends is consequently more important than short-term measurement of absolute values. Process tracking supports the collection and correlation of estimated time, cost, and schedule data with the actual performance of a process, and tracks items to closure. It may provide triggers or alarms when actual data varies outside predefined limits of resource usage, event milestones, backlogs or queues, and cycle times.

Audit trails track financial value.

An audit trail is a kind of *process monitoring* that tracks the flow of monetary value in a financial ledger. Figure 3-5 illustrates how an assembly process debits the product inventory account, and credits its process account, with the product value. The cost of material is credited to component inventory accounts and debited to the process account, and the balance remaining in the process account is the value added by the process. This approach supports activity-based

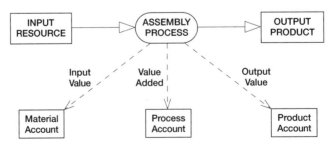

Figure 3-5 Value Added by Process

costing (ABC), because the ABC cost is the sum of the costs of the resources used by the various process steps, and the process account records added value. This accounting model is one aspect of the more general business model, and accounts measure purpose only from the accounting point of view.

Process Design with UML

A business process has complex responsibilities, including its definition, instantiation, workflow, security, documentation, and user interfaces. Fortunately, most of these requirements are shared by all processes, and so may be implemented in a generic process from which others are derived. As yet, however, there is no universal agreement on process and workflow ideas, let alone standards. However, some concepts are gaining acceptance through the efforts of the Object Management Group (OMG) and the Workflow Management Coalition (WfMC). In particular, an understanding of the relationships among business use cases, business processes, and workflow is emerging.

Business process objects have complex responsibilities.

Business Use Case

The broad requirements of a business process may be elicited and documented with *use cases*. Use case models describe what is required of a system by defining how it will be used by external actors. An actor, which is usually but not necessarily human, causes the system to perform its functions by means of use cases. A business use case may be thought of as a collection of related process steps, and actors may be thought of as the organization roles that execute the process steps. Because a business process defines how a purpose is to be achieved, a business use case should also be directed to satisfy a business purpose.

Use cases help define specific business processes.

When a business use case is directed to a particular purpose, its intent and scope are well defined, avoiding many kinds of problems that are otherwise encountered. If the scope is too broad, its purpose should be refined and focused using the concepts described in Chapter 2. Conversely, if the use case is too narrow or sparse, a more substantial (higher) purpose should be selected to define its scope. This is illustrated in Figure 3-6 for an extremely simple sales process, the purpose of which is to sell goods or services to customers. Descriptions of more comprehensive use cases are available in the relevant literature [Jacobson et al. 1999], [Rosenberg 1999], [Schneider and Winters 1998].

A process step is modeled by a use case and its actors.

Each step in the process is represented by a use case and the actor(s) who use it. In the example, shown in Figure 3-6, the process is initiated by a sales inquiry from a customer, to which the supplier responds with a quotation. This in turn may result in an order from the customer, and subsequent delivery and invoicing by the supplier. While this is a very simple use case, it has captured some important information about the sales process. First, the process has four distinct steps—inquire, quote, order, and deliver—each of which is separated from the others in space and time.

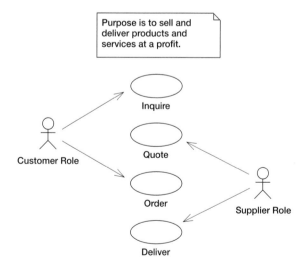

Figure 3-6 Business Use Case

Second, the process involves two distinct kinds of actors—a customer and a supplier—who play different roles with respect to the process. Note that the diagram does not show any dependencies between use cases, although it is likely that an inquiry precedes a quotation, a quotation precedes an order, and so on. Dependencies between use cases define the expected flow of business events, which may be formalized into workflow rules. These rules can be quite complex, involving conditional branching and synchronization of multiple threads. Since one of the main purposes of a use case is to facilitate communication between users and developers, it should reflect only the essential aspects of a process. Workflow can be both complex and dynamic, and so it is usually not appropriate to model workflow with use cases.

Use cases help users and developers communicate.

Process States

The WfMC has proposed a process model that has at its heart a standard *state transition diagram*. The set of process states illustrated in Figure 3-7 conforms to these standards, but may be augmented

A process is activated when it is selected by an actor.

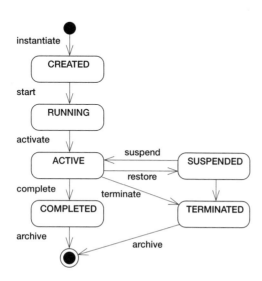

Figure 3-7 Standard Process States

to satisfy the specific needs of a particular business process. A process is not available for work when it is enacted, but must first be started by the process manager. When its workflow start or join conditions are satisfied, the process is transferred into the work queue of the role responsible for its execution. The process is activated when selected by an actor having the role, typically from a *worklist* or in-tray. The process can be suspended from, and restored to, the active state by the actor. No work can be done on the process while it is suspended. It may also be terminated from its active or suspended state, in which case work may never again be done on the process. In the normal course of affairs, the process will be completed, during which it will update the entities, ledgers, and data warehouses with which it interacts. These updates are also normally committed to a persistent state by the complete action. Finally, the process is archived and cannot be used any further.

Process states should not be extended to model business steps.

One way to model the dependencies within a process is to extend the standard process state diagram to handle specialized events. For example, one might want to include a delayed state in which the process is suspended for a period of time before being restored to the active state. However, the states should not be extended to model logical steps within a process. For example, a sales process might have steps for inquiry, quotation, order, and invoice, with options to reject the quotation, cancel the order, and pass a credit note, as illustrated in Figure 3-8.

Steps should be modeled by sub-classing the process.

While it is tempting to implement steps as a set of states in a single process, there are several reasons why one should take a more sophisticated approach. First, one almost certainly needs a record of the process at each step for auditing and tracking purposes. Second, the events to which the process can respond change, depending on the state it is in. For example, one cannot cancel a sale that has been invoiced, or pass a credit note against one that has not yet been invoiced. Third, it is likely that each of these steps will be performed by different roles at different times. Finally, in a distributed system,

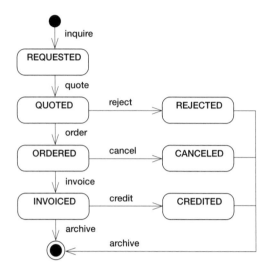

Figure 3-8   Sales Process Steps

it is quite likely that the steps in a process will be executed by different people at different locations, so require separate instances.

Activity Diagram

The activity diagram in UML is a specialization of a state diagram
intended to model business processes. In the context of a business
process, an activity is a discrete step that may be related to other
activities by a network of dependencies. The result is a clear notation that is comprehensible to management and users and sufficiently precise to implement workflow-enabled processes. While
use case diagrams are good for capturing basic requirements, the
more formal activity notation is needed to document process
dependencies. Business processes are typically designed and re-
engineered by business people rather than by technologists, so the
process notation should be oriented toward business rather than
technological needs.

*A process notation is
for management and
users.*

The core elements of an activity diagram are listed in Figure 3-9, using
business process and workflow terminology. Swimlanes separate

*Activity diagrams
replace flowcharts.*

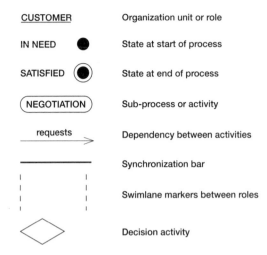

Figure 3-9 Process Notation

activities performed by different organization units and roles. Process flow occurs between roles within a unit, and may occur between units using business messages. The bullet and target symbols indicating the start and end of a process are equivalent to the start and end states of a state diagram. Each activity or subprocess is represented by an oval, equivalent to a state in a state diagram, and is dependent on other activities in much the same way as the states are related by transitions. Finally, decision activities and synchronization bars enable conditional and parallel workflows to be modeled.

Flowcharts are understood by non-technical users.

While object purists may object to the *flowchart* flavor of an activity diagram, that is <u>exactly</u> the characteristic that makes it accessible to nontechnical managers and users. This notation is used to illustrate the simple sequential sales process in Figure 3-10. Note that the activities are assigned to roles that correspond to the actors in the use case diagram, and are in swimlanes separated by the dashed vertical line. A diagram that has activities partitioned between roles in this way is a role activity diagram.

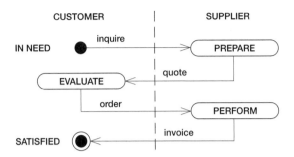

Figure 3-10   Role Activity Diagram

Role Activity Diagram

Scenarios were originally adopted to help managers evaluate different alternative paths into the future—particularly with respect to
changing business environments. They have been further applied
by Booch, Jacobson, and others to help model the use of objects in
information systems. Jacobson [Jacobson et al. 1995], Booch
[Booch 1994], and Senge [Senge 1990] use the term "scenario" to
describe an instance of a use case or business process, albeit with
somewhat different emphasis. Scenarios and use cases may be formalized into properly defined business processes that specify not
only the possible uses of the system, but also the constraints and
rules under which it may be used.

*Scenarios evaluate
alternative process
paths.*

The UML activity diagram notation, organized into columns for
each participating organization unit or role, is used to describe processes. The role activity diagram models the interaction between
different actors, including the customer, in a business process (see
Figure 3-11). It illustrates the flow of work (in oval boxes), done by
different roles (in columns between vertical dotted lines) via the
events that cause them to interact (indicated by horizontal arrows).
Organization roles are defined at the top of each role column. The
process start and end states are indicated by solid and concentric
circles, respectively.

*The UML activity
diagram is organized
by role.*

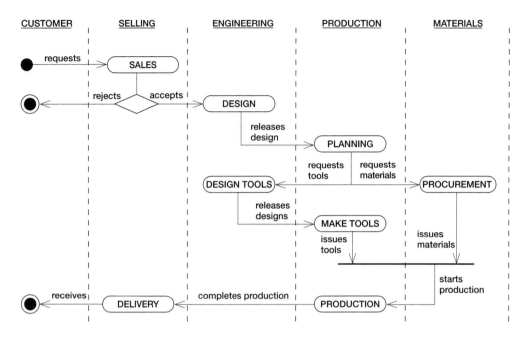

Figure 3-11 Complex Activity Diagram

The example illustrates a make-to-order process.

This example is a simple illustration of a make-to-order process. The sales division negotiates an order with the customer, requests that the design be done by the engineering division, and requests that the production be planned by the production division. The production division calculates the material required and requests it from the materials division, which arranges for its procurement, and so on. The heavy horizontal line is a synchronization bar that indicates that both the materials procurement and tool manufacturing processes must be completed before product manufacturing can begin.

Managing Process Complexity

A business process may be too complex to be represented clearly on a single diagram.

A business process may be too complex to be represented clearly on a single diagram, in which case it should be decomposed into a number of simpler diagrams. Several process activities are replaced by a single subprocess, which is in turn represented by a separate process diagram. Process definitions may be decomposed to an arbitrary number of levels in this way. Decomposition is typically used to hide the complexity of rarely used "exceptional" process flows, for handling large processes such as construction projects, and for providing overview process diagrams.

Figure 3-12 illustrates how a single subprocess—in this case the procurement process—is exploded into a diagram of its own. The ability to add detail progressively through subprocesses allows one to manage the complexity of individual activity diagrams. It also allows reuse of standard patterns of activity during creation of a new process. For example, an authorization activity that is used in a variety of processes might not need to be different for each process. Indeed, it is quite feasible to establish a library of common activity types that can be reused from process to process [Malone 1996].

A process can be composed of other processes.

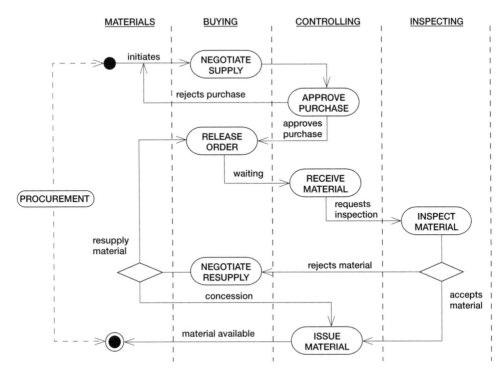

Figure 3-12 Process Decomposition

Processes are decoupled by intermediate artifacts.

Another way to simplify a complex process is to decouple it into two or more processes connected through some kind of artifact (see Figures 3-13 and 3-14). This is often the case in manufacturing, where inventories of intermediate components and assemblies decouple fabrication processes from assembly. Such simplification does not come without cost, however, because the processes must now be coordinated to ensure that there is sufficient, yet not excessive, inventory. Traditional material requirements planning performs this function by partitioning a complex process into simple linear routings to make items that are assembled into products guided by their bills of material.

A work breakdown structure decomposes projects.

Process and project management environments, and just-in-time manufacturing, tend not to rely on inventory for decoupling of process activities. Large projects are decomposed into deliverable elements by means of a work breakdown structure (WBS). Each element is delivered by a process, sometimes called a subproject, while the interaction between processes is minimized. Coordination of these processes is achieved by planning and tracking WBS milestones, rather than by scheduling each activity in detail. Naturally, organizations responsible for delivery of each WBS element are likely to schedule their own processes to meet their commitments.

Kanbans decouple processes.

Work is similarly coordinated in just-in-time systems, but activities are decoupled by artifacts such as *kanban* bins or cards instead of by inventory. Just as a kanban card signals a requirement to a supplier, other messages can communicate interesting business events, which in turn initiate processes. Although it is tempting to think of this as a single process, there are subtle differences between the integrated process illustrated in Figure 3-13 and the interacting processes shown in Figure 3-15. The integrated process assumes that it is conducted under a single authority, and so can be managed explicitly.

Interacting processes have no single authority.

The interacting processes are subject to no single authority, and so must coordinate their activities according to an explicit business agreement, or contract. Although the physical message can take

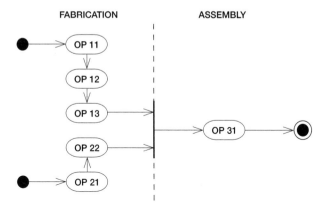

Figure 3-13   Coupled Process

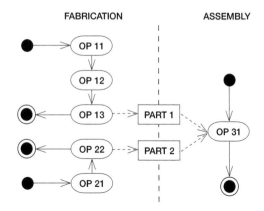

Figure 3-14   Decoupled Processes

any form, from paper document through electronic function call, its content must comply with agreed standards for such communication to be successful. Therefore, its design cannot be delegated to a lower-level information, computation, or communication layer, but is an explicit part of the enterprise model. The inventory and messages in these examples occur when each subprocess has achieved its purpose, and so Figure 3-15 can be amended to reflect the contract states that link them, as shown in Figure 3-16.

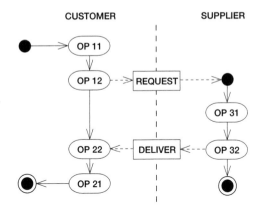

Figure 3-15   Interacting Processes

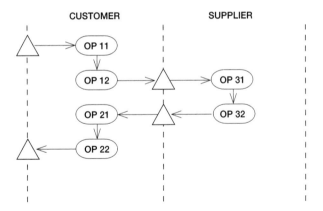

Figure 3-16   Coupled by Purpose

The processes are now equivalent to the transitions in a contract diagram (see Contract Components on page 159). While this may not appear to be a very useful distinction, it highlights the legal transactions that occur between the units and the fact that achievement of preceding purpose is a *precondition* to the processes. It is a distinction that can now be introduced between workflow within an organization and interaction between organizations (Figure 3-17).

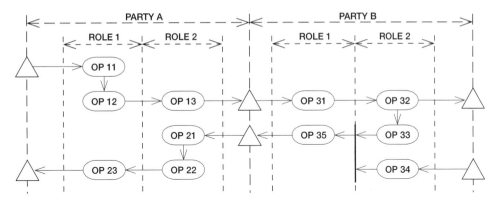

Figure 3-17 Workflow and Interaction

The individual operations between roles within an organization do not necessarily have to achieve a purpose, but collectively they must achieve a purpose between parties. This is a business <u>design</u> decision that may not hold for all organizations and situations but that helps illustrate the difference between process flow within and between organizations. Naturally, other approaches are also feasible and reasonable. For example, each process step might have a purpose; alternatively, conventional workflow might be used between parties. The example illustrated in Figure 3-17 is typical of value chain processes, in which communication of messages, governed by contracts, coordinates work between parties.

Contracts coordinate work between parties.

Process Sequence Diagram

An atomic process step uses and modifies the state of associated entities, and posts to ledgers and data warehouses (see Process Steps on page 54). The interaction between a process step and other business objects is well illustrated by a UML sequence diagram. A sequence diagram specifies how a client object—the process step—uses the services of other objects, by illustrating its sequence, branching and looping, exceptions, and side effects. This kind of sequence diagram should not attempt to probe the behavior of the objects, but to describe how they collaborate during the process step.

An activity interacts with other objects through actions.

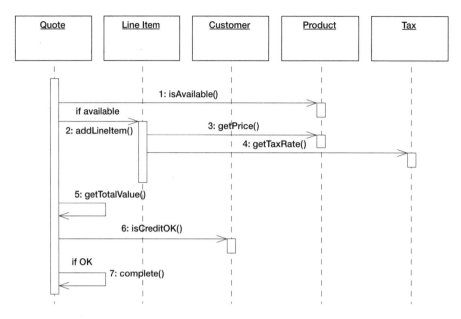

Figure 3-18 Sequence Diagram

Partition process and entity to improve reusability and flexibility.

A process step may also be modeled by an activity diagram, just as a complete process may be represented by a sequence diagram. However, because a process step is performed by a single organization role, only the entity properties for that role need be modeled and instantiated. This encourages the process designer to use role-based modeling, which helps manage complexity, increase reuse, and improve efficiency (see Entity Properties on page 92). By using an atomic process step at its boundary, the business process model is cleanly separated from the business entity model. This in turn enables the benefits of a stable and reusable entity model to be combined with those of a flexible and adaptable process model.

Process Components

All processes share some behavior.

The behavior described in the preceding sections applies to all processes, and thus can be implemented by a generic process—an *abstract class*—from which specific business processes inherit. A business

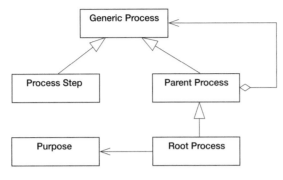

Figure 3-19   Generic Process

process is fractal, having subprocesses containing, at the lowest level, discrete process steps (see Compound Processes on page 56).

A root process is a special case that is created at the start of a process to manage the aspects shared by the whole process. For example, the root process knows its goal purpose, which is the obligation that caused it to be enacted, and which it fulfills when satisfactorily completed. It also knows the obligations that are created when it fails to achieve its goal, perhaps because it is canceled, or because it violates its governing contract. Preconditions are goals that must have been achieved before the process can start, which are strongly reminiscent of the milestones of project environments. They relate to any situation in which purpose is shared, and are particularly useful in distributed value chains.

A root process is created when an obligation is incurred.

Every step in the process knows its root, and is known to its root. This enables the root process to apply business and housekeeping rules to all its members. For example, a manufacturing process may have many subprocesses that refer to the root process to consolidate costs, to determine the job, and for scheduling purposes. A master schedule is a prioritized list of production obligations, each instantiating a root process, while detailed schedules reference their individual steps. When a root process is deleted, it must check that each

Every step in the process knows its root, and is known to its root.

of its steps is in an acceptable state, and take appropriate action if it is not.

Instantiate a new process for each step.

A new object is instantiated for each process step, and its information is copied or cloned to the new step. Each process step records the time and date on which it was done, its effective time and date, by whom it was done, and the entities that it consumed and produced. This represents a "snapshot" of the process at each step, and allows it to remain where it was executed. Subsequent steps are also instances that record similar information at different stages of the process. A sales inquiry specifies the prospective customer and the products, quantities, and due dates that are required. A quotation adds prices per item with totals, perhaps including sales tax. An order might indicate the quantity for immediate delivery, the quantity on back order, and the lost sale quantity (see Figure 3-20).

Operations vary for each process step.

Process operations also vary between each step. All processes support standard operations such as start, activate, suspend, restore, complete, and terminate. The root sales process also has an operation to create a quotation process step, which in turn has operations to accept or reject the quotation. Only those operations that relate to the current process step are available at any time. Note that in this scheme, the preceding process is responsible to instantiate its successor. This has particular benefit if user interface and process documentation is automatically created, where the process document and its menu options directly reflect the attributes and operations of the process object. Document details and operations vary as the process is executed, typically building up information step by step.

Basic Process Class

A simple activity involves few entities.

The basic process class records information about a simple activity that involves few, if any, entities. For example, a process to schedule and track the contact between a sales representative and a prospective customer needs only to record the representative, the customer, the date and time, and a textual description of the meeting.

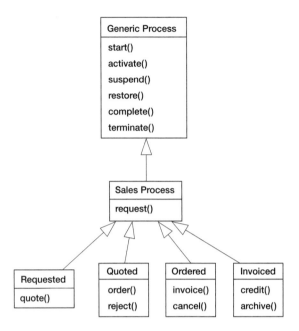

Figure 3-20 Sales Process

Most of this information is common to all processes, and so is defined in the generic process class (Figure 3-21). The reference is an optional code by which the process is identified. Note that the start date on which the process is entered into the system is not necessarily the same as the effective date, which is when the process actually took place. The role identifies the organization role that is responsible for the process, and the actor is the actual person or other entity to which it is assigned. These attributes are extended by the contact process to include references to the specific representative and customer involved in, and a description of, the meeting.

This example is unusually simple because it has no scheduling, entity usage, accounting, or other such behavior. Most processes are designed to help plan and track events that affect the entities of an organization. The interaction between the process and the entities is critical information. For example, a sales process records the sale of goods

Most processes affect entities.

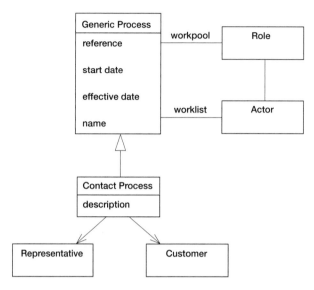

Figure 3-21   Contact Process

or services to a customer, and a manufacturing process tracks the materials, labor, equipment, and other input entities and the products that it produces. This type of process is known as an order, as in sales order, purchase order, production or work order, and so on.

Cash Sale Process

A cash sale process exchanges product for cash.

A simple process exchanges one kind of entity for another, such as a sale of product for cash, in which a cash price is paid for a quantity of product. The process in this example has two methods. The first is a precondition that checks that the product and bank account are defined, and that the quantity is greater than zero, before the process can be completed. The second records the issue of the product and the deposit of the cash in the bank or other account (Figure 3-22). The complete method may also verify the *invariant* and *postcondition* to check that the step has been performed correctly, otherwise raising an exception. It then calls the complete method of the generic process to change the workflow state of the process to completed and to remove the process step from the *workpool*.

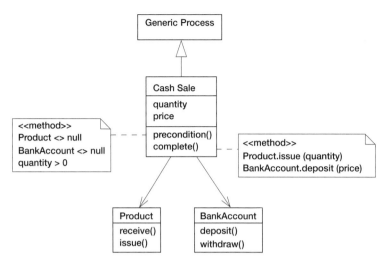

Figure 3-22   Cash Sale Process

While the product and bank account entities may themselves
account, respectively, for the flow of value caused by the issue and
deposit operations, this responsibility is often delegated to a separate ledger. An advantage of posting directly from the process to
such a ledger is that accounts may vary according to the process
context, and may change for different organizations, process types,
and so on. It also enables the process to enforce business rules to
ensure that the values posted sum to zero, are to the same period,
and relate to the same transaction. Naturally, the ledger and the
posting methods are associated with a generic process class as they
are potentially used by any process that has financial effects.

*A generic process
may enforce generic
business rules.*

Multiple-Item Process

A more typical process involves interaction with more than one
entity in a single step, each of which is recorded in a list of line
items contained in the process. The example of a purchase order
process is an exchange between a supplier and inventory, in which
the supplier is credited with the value of the inventory. The value of
the product is summarized from the value of each line item by the
method `totalPrice()`, and is credited to the supplier by means of

*A typical process
involves more than
one entity.*

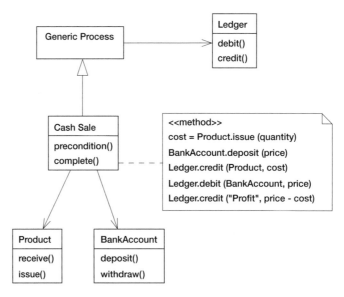

Figure 3-23 Cash Sale with Accounting

its `buy()` method. Each line item updates the appropriate product object by its `receive()` method, which is called by the `complete()` method in the purchase process (see Figure 3-24). Note that the `precondition()` and `complete()` methods in the process invoke their equivalent methods for each line item.

Process steps handle differences in input and output values and timing.

In this example it is assumed that the supplier is credited at the same time as the inventory is received so that there is no accounting inconsistency. However, there is often a difference between the product cost and the purchase price, and also a timing difference between receipt of the goods and receipt of the supplier's invoice. This is handled by process steps that debit the process account when products are received, and credit it when the invoice is processed (see Figure 3-25). The cost at which the product is received may be different from the invoiced price, resulting in a nonzero process value. The difference is normally treated as a purchase price variance to avoid having to adjust retrospectively the value of product inventory, and is posted when the invoice step is completed.

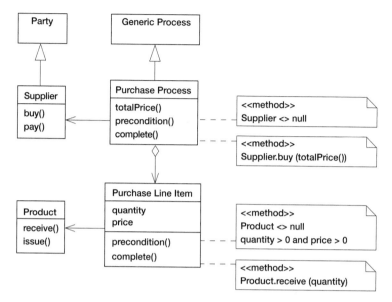

Figure 3-24   Purchase Process

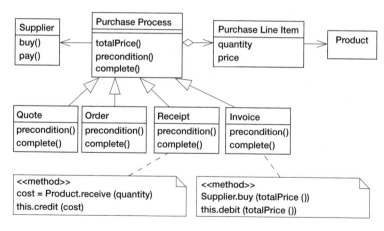

Figure 3-25   Purchase Process Steps

Process Value Added

A similar situation exists in a sales process, where the cost of goods sold is hopefully lower than the price to be invoiced. In the example shown in Figure 3-26, the sales process has steps for recording

Output value minus input cost is value added.

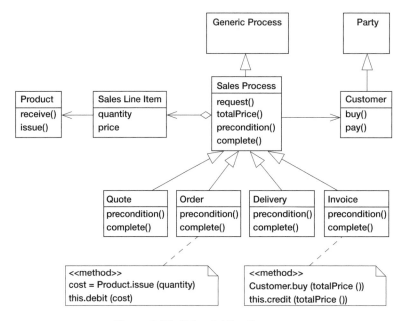

Figure 3-26   Value-Adding Process

when the products are quoted, ordered, delivered, and invoiced. The process account is debited with the cost of product when delivered, and credited with the sales value when invoiced. The difference is the gross profit of the sale, which is also (arguably) the value added by the process. This technique may be used to determine where value is added by any process in a value chain, and to monitor actual against standard added value, which in turn is the basis of activity-based costing.

Work in Process

Work in process objects help manage long-duration processes.

Many processes are of relatively long duration, particularly in engineering, manufacturing, and project environments. Activity during the interval between the start and completion of such a process is known as *work in process* (WIP). A process that has finite duration typically has one or more subsidiary process steps for recording its WIP activities. Because WIP in effect models a long transaction, it requires a set of atomic process steps that schedule and record significant

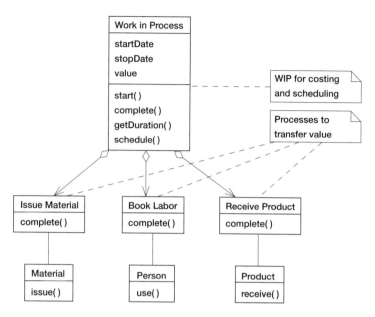

Figure 3-27   Work in Process

events in its progress; otherwise, the state of entities affected by the process would have to be locked to preserve their integrity. This is not feasible for resources that are shared among many processes, which is typical in business. Most operational systems have process steps that record the issue of materials and parts, the receipt of products, and the use of labor, equipment, and tools. Sophisticated systems also have processes for recording by-products, waste, lost time, breakdowns, and other occurrences that affect WIP.

Values of a process having zero duration may be accounted for by crediting input costs, debiting the output value, and posting the difference to a value added account (see Process Monitoring on page 61). However, applying this approach to WIP having nonzero duration causes the financial ledger to be out of balance between its start and completion. Instead, input values are debited, and output values are credited, to the WIP by its subprocess steps. Before the WIP is completed, the net balance of these values is posted to an

Value is transformed from input resources to output entities.

appropriate account to ensure that its residual value is zero. This is typically called a profit or loss on WIP, or a production or project variance.

WIP may not be completed before subsidiary processes.

Completion of a WIP process is somewhat different from that of an atomic process step, because its subsidiary process steps must also be completed. The simplest strategy is to recursively check that all subsidiary processes have completed before the WIP is allowed to complete. An alternative method is to complete automatically the subsidiary processes as part of the operation that completes the WIP. This approach is equivalent to the *backflush* operation found in MRP systems, but should be used with care to prevent the incorrect completion of pending processes. A third approach is to terminate all incomplete subsidiary processes prior to completing the WIP, which implies that the processes were never started. The most common approach, however, is to list the subsidiary processes that are incomplete and to complete or terminate them individually before completing the WIP.

WIP models processes of finite duration.

WIP exists in many forms, ranging from projects, jobs, and discrete assembly to flow manufacturing and service processes, as illustrated by the taxonomy in Figure 3-28. The abstract generic process class has finite duration, which is determined by recording its start and completion. The `schedule()` operation calculates the process stop date from its start date and `getDuration()` operation. The duration may be implemented as an attribute in a simple system. However, process duration is often dynamic, depending on the availability and capacity of resources, which require a more sophisticated implementation.

Discrete WIP models discrete assembly processes.

The discrete WIP class extends the generic process class for discrete manufacturing processes, such as the fabrication and assembly of products from component parts and materials. A WIP object represents one or more operations executed in a sequence, to convert input materials, tools, labor, and other resources into output product.

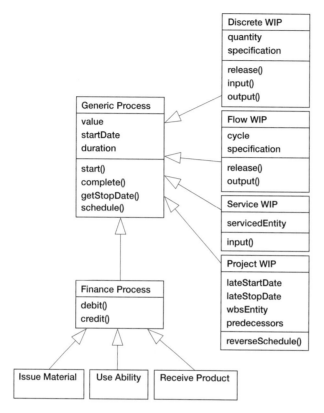

Figure 3-28   WIP Options

The output of the operation may be an intermediate product such as a part, subassembly, or partially finished item. Because each item is discrete, the WIP quantity can be calculated as the difference between the input and output quantities of the process. This information is used to verify physical WIP in much the same way as physical inventory is verified.

Flow WIP objects model continuous manufacturing processes in which discrete products are difficult or impossible to identify. These processes are typical of chemical, petroleum, food, mining, and some just-in-time manufacturing industries. WIP is planned and monitored according to production cycles, which typically are time

Flow WIP objects model continuous manufacturing processes.

intervals such as hours or shifts, but which also can be based on any other convenient batching scheme. The cycle of a blending process, for example, might be dictated by the size of the primary blending vessel. The output of each cycle is scheduled and measured, and the input can then be calculated because WIP quantities tend not to vary significantly in flow processes. Flow processes typically back-flush input resources by multiplying measured outputs by standard quantities and rates.

A service process does not have a tangible output.

Service WIP objects model the work required to perform services, including transport, maintenance, development, travel, entertainment, consulting, and many other processes that have intangible outputs. Their primary task is to schedule resources and collect costs. The `input()` operation records the human and other resources used to perform the service. The `complete()` operation implies that the service has been performed, because it is not feasible to measure directly the output of a service process. The operation typically invoices a customer, updates the service cost of a maintained item, or posts a development cost to the appropriate financial account.

Projects are modeled by networks of activities.

Project WIP objects model the activities required by construction, engineering, and large-scale manufacturing projects, typically having complex networks of interdependent tasks. The network topology is defined by the predecessor activities of each, which enables the reverse scheduling of late start and end dates, in addition to the forward scheduling of early dates implemented in the generic process. This in turn enables critical path analysis, resource balancing, time/cost trade-offs, and other project management functions. Each project activity may also have a deliverable item specified in the work breakdown structure, which is used to contract and measure progress.

A finance process enforces accounting rules.

The second set of operational processes derives from an abstract finance process, typically designed to model the subsidiary processes of a WIP. A finance process has financial implications that are accounted for in a ledger by means of `debit()` and `credit()` operations. Because a finance process is atomic, the values posted by these operations must sum to zero; otherwise, the ledger does not remain in balance. The process tests for this condition before it is completed, and raises an exception if not satisfied. Each WIP object has a set of transactions for recording the issue of components and the receipt of product and for tracking the progress of operations. Other transactions monitor process waste such as lost time, damaged components, breakdowns, accidents, and other incidents that affect WIP.

Process Folders

Certain types of processes require unstructured information to be accumulated, modified, and carried between process steps. Examples include insurance claims, medical cases, employee selection processes, and so on. The concept of a folder that can contain any document related to the process is used to support this type of process. The model is surprisingly similar to an order process, which may be thought of as a folder having a document for each line item (Figure 3-29). Since each process step inherits from the root process, any document added during a process step is available to subsequent process steps. This is the equivalent of passing a physical folder containing the documents between the case workers

Processes need information to be carried between steps.

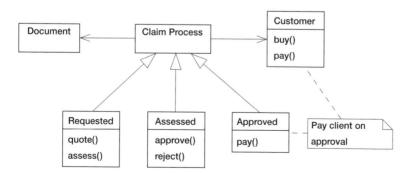

Figure 3-29 Claim Process

involved in the process. The process is easily extended to allow a folder to contain other folders to model hierarchical documents.

Summary

A business process has many definitions, but there is broad consensus that it must add value to the enterprise and its customers. Most processes are comprised of several related steps, each assigned to an organizational role and performed by an actor having that role. Workflow is the means by which the activities of a process are routed to actors according to the process state and the actors' roles.

Business processes are defined with varying degrees of flexibility and precision, from unstructured ad hoc processes to precisely defined production processes. They may be represented in several ways using UML, but role activity diagrams are generally sufficient for workflow, security, and other purposes. General and specific performance measures and standards are part of a process definition, and relate to measures of the purpose of the process.

Business processes may be implemented in many ways, and the proposed approach enables most process functionality to be implemented in abstract types. This promotes significant reuse of generic concepts and code, including user interfaces, workflow, transaction management, and security. Specific process steps are implemented with ease by extending generic processes.

The complexity of enterprise systems is significantly reduced by implementing them with standard reusable components coupled by flexible business processes. This approach enables business engineers to design and implement custom business processes with minimal understanding of the underlying technologies.

4

Entities

An entity is created, used, and destroyed by business processes, and is modeled by the roles that it plays with respect to those processes. A role depends on the context in which it is used, but its values are independent of that context. It has a set of roles for interacting with processes, and a set of values for modeling its state. Roles are reusable between processes, and values are reusable among entities and organizations.

Entity Models

Entities are the things created and used by business processes in order to add value and thereby achieve purpose. Most entities are physical things such as people, machines, vehicles, materials, and products. Less tangible entities, such as designs, specifications, and business partners, are also of value to an organization. Much of the knowledge of an enterprise is represented in the models of such entities—for example, the features, prices, costs, structure, and quality of products; the abilities and capacities of machines, tools, manpower, and suppliers; the quantities and locations of inventories; and the preferences and demands of consumers.

Entities are created and used by processes.

An entity typically fulfills several roles with respect to various organizations, depending on the processes in which it is used. A person might be an employee, a father, a member of a sports team, and a licensed driver of motor vehicles—each of which is a role that he or she plays. This helps to simplify a model by partitioning it into separate but related aspects or areas of concern. A particular process is typically interested only in one aspect of an entity [Reenskaug 1996]. For example, a motor vehicle might be an asset in a capital expenditure process, a resource in a transport process, and a maintenance

An entity may fulfill many roles.

item in a service process. Human users are also entities that can perform roles with respect to processes. A particular individual might be able to develop software, manage projects, and make technical presentations, each a distinct role.

Entity Properties

Complex objects are modeled by collections of properties.

An entity may be modeled as a composition of properties, each of which is also an object, but at a different level of abstraction (see Entities on page 9). The properties are dynamic, being attached and detached as required to model an entity in various contexts and at different times. They are broadly classified as follows.

- *Roles* for modeling aspects of the entity's external behavior

- *Values* for modeling the entity's inherent qualities and abilities

For example, a particular company might be modeled by the collection of roles it can assume, such as customer, supplier, and employer, and by a set of values, such as physical, postal, and electronic addresses. It has the role of customer in a sales process and the role of supplier in a purchasing process. An address is valid in both its customer and supplier roles.

Roles and values are properties.

Reenskaug recognizes this differentiation in answering his question "What is a good object?" by stating that a good business object is typically:

- A model of a part of the real world

- A thing to which thought or action is directed

- An entity in an entity-relationship model

- Something that has identity and exists over time

Entities have roles and values.

An entity interacts with a process through one or more of its external roles, and the roles in turn reference its internal values. In the

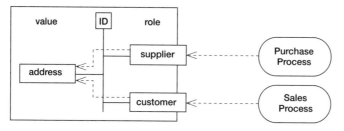

Figure 4-1 Entity Properties

example illustrated in Figure 4-1, a purchasing process does not access the address directly, but requests the address from the supplier role, which in turn accesses the address value. The same entity has a customer role, which accesses the address value in the context of a sales process. Should the entity at some time need different addresses for sales and purchasing, the change is localized to the entity itself, and does not affect the processes in which it is used.

The role of an entity is relative to a context, and its identity is a name that is unique in that context. The entity has different roles in other contexts, which are linked by a globally unique internal identity. Indeed, one might argue that an entity initially has only its global identity, to which properties are appended to provide the behavior that gives it meaning. This approach enables an entity to "learn and grow" progressively as it adopts the roles that it is expected to perform. For example, one might model the first contact with a company as a new entity having a consumer role and an address value, as illustrated in Figure 4-2.

The role of an entity is relative to a context.

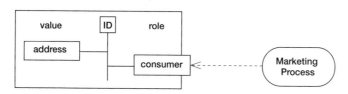

Figure 4-2 Initial Contact

A sales process might result in the company becoming a customer, which
requires credit control, sales, and other information about the company,
in addition to the consumer-related information (see Figure 4-3).

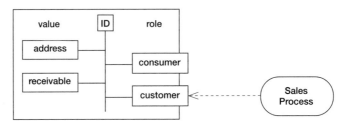

Figure 4-3   New Customer

The company might then provide goods or services, and so become
a supplier, requiring additional information such as price lists, lead
times, payment terms, and conditions of supply (see Figure 4-4).
An accounts payable property might also be added in the same way
as receivables were added for the customer role, or one might
choose to merge both into a single control account.

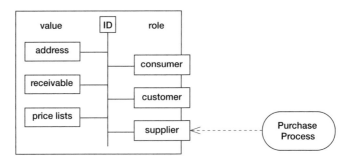

Figure 4-4   Purchase from Supplier

The relationship with the company might develop further into a
partnership or alliance supported by agreements, technology and
staff exchanges, and other aspects of which knowledge must be
obtained and maintained (see Figure 4-5).

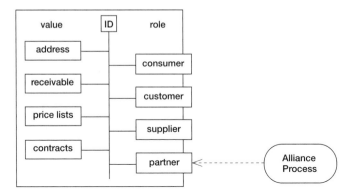

Figure 4-5   Negotiate with Partner

The partnership may eventually result in the company being acquired, so that it becomes a subsidiary. The shareholding and other acquisition details would be required, and the entity might become a different legal party (see Figure 4-6). Note that the information added by each process need not have been envisioned when the entity was originally created.

The company may be acquired.

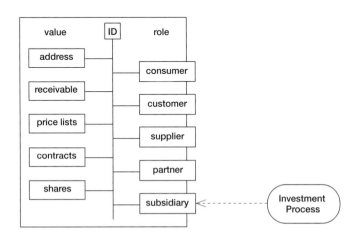

Figure 4-6   Acquire Subsidiary

A property added by a process may be used by other processes.

These scenarios illustrate how information about an entity may be built up (and trimmed) as the need arises. Each property is added by a business process, and may be used by other processes. A process for adding the customer creates the customer role and values for its accounts, personnel and contacts, and marketing information. A sales process may then use the customer role for credit control, contact management, and sales tracking. Other processes add, use, and remove properties during the life cycle of the entity, which may be modeled from many points of view.

Alternative Models

Entities are modeled by roles and values.

A complex entity that is typical of business systems is often difficult to model with a single class, because it tends to be used in many different ways, and its structure and behavior change over time. The section Entity Properties on page 92 describes how these issues are handled by role and value properties. While the approach is conceptually straightforward, there are many ways in which the issues can be modeled, each of which has advantages and disadvantages [Fowler 1997A].

Fowler proposes the following five alternatives (see Figure 4-7).

Roles can be modeled in several ways.

- Combine all the features into a single type.

- Treat each role as a separate type.

- Put common behavior in a supertype, with a subtype for each role.

- Put common behavior in a host object, with a separate object for each role.

- Make each role a relationship with an appropriate object.

Each is a trade-off between simplicity and power.

The first alternative appears simple, but can lead to complexity for multifaceted business entities. The second alternative enables many facets to be modeled, but has no systematic way of unifying the

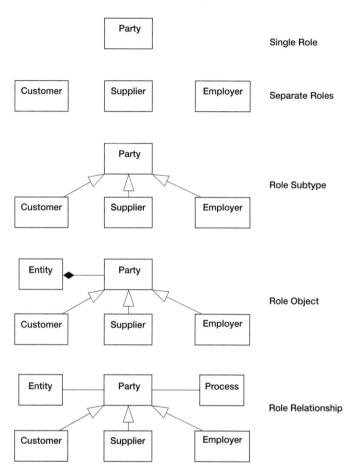

Figure 4-7   Alternative Models

shared properties and global identity of an entity. Objects of the third type share identity between roles, but need to be able to add new roles at runtime. This feature is not supported directly by any mainstream object-oriented language, and so must be explicitly implemented by an application or framework.

The next alternative is to use composition instead of inheritance, and to attach separate role objects to the entity as they are required. A client asks the entity for the appropriate role, and then interacts

Entities can be synthesized from their roles.

with that role directly. In effect, the entity adds a second level of indirection between the client and the server objects. Finally, each role can be modeled as a relationship between the entity and some other object. This has the advantage that the other object provides a context for defining the services that the role is to provide. It may result in duplication of services, however, if many similar relationships are required.

Entity Roles and Values

A primitive entity has only its global identity.

The approach adopted in this chapter uses aspects of these patterns, extended to enable the widest possible reuse of component objects. A core entity has only its identity, and its purpose is to link its roles, which model its external interface, to other roles, and to value objects, which model its behavior and state. An entity role is designed for a particular context, which in turn is defined by the processes that it is to service. This is not to say that every process is served by a different role, but that each role serves the needs of a set of similar processes. Because an entity is a composition of its properties, when it is deleted, its properties are also deleted (see Figure 4-8).

Each describes an aspect of an entity.

Figure 4-9 is an attempt to illustrate by example the different kinds of entities identified in the enterprise metamodel (see Enterprise Metamodel on page 21). A party may contract, for example, as a

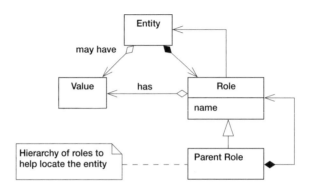

Figure 4-8   Roles and Values

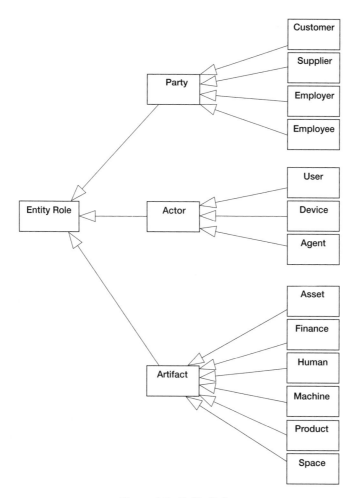

Figure 4-9   Entity Roles

customer, supplier, employer, or employee. An actor may be a
human user, an electronic device, or a software agent. Artifacts
include the things that are created and used by processes, such as
products, people, machines, space, and finance. A single entity can
play any number of these roles: a person might be a party to an
employment agreement (employee role), a user responsible for a
process (actor role), and a resource in that and other processes
(artifact role).

Values are entity building blocks.

Values are the building blocks or components with which knowledge of an entity is constructed. They typically describe well-understood and reusable packages of behavior, and so are ideal candidates for standardization within and between organizations. Value properties are not used directly by processes, but through entity roles. This may appear clumsy for a simple model but is valuable when the entity is required to play multiple roles and when additional properties are to be added during its life cycle.

Roles describe what an entity is, values list what it has and does.

Figure 4-10 lists various kinds of entity values, broadly categorized, to illustrate their characteristics. An address, for example, enables one to locate an entity physically, by post, geographically, or electronically. The useful capacity of an entity may be consumed if it is cash or inventory, may be monopolized if it is a machine or tool, or may be accessed if it is a document or other information resource (see Capacity on page 121). Various kinds of accounts record and audit the financial value of an entity, and other attributes reflect its abilities, preferences, qualities, and dimensions. This classification may be both limited and arbitrary, but it highlights the difference between the roles and values of an entity. A role describes what the entity <u>is</u>, while values list what it <u>has</u> and <u>does</u>.

Names and Identity of an Entity

RM-ODP precisely defines distributed object concepts.

The ISO Reference Model for Open Distributed Processing (RM-ODP) describes a role as an identifier for a behavior that is associated with a component of a composite object [ISO/IEC 10746-1 1995]. RM-ODP goes further to define a name as the unambiguous identity of an object in a naming context. In this chapter, a role both identifies and describes a behavior of the entity, in a particular business context, from the RM-ODP enterprise *viewpoint*. Business contexts are closely related to business processes, and tend to vary between domains and organizations.

The identity of an entity is relative to an organization role.

The choice of context is subjective, depending on how the entity is used. Entities are used in business processes, so contexts tend to be aligned with particular kinds of processes—such as sales, marketing,

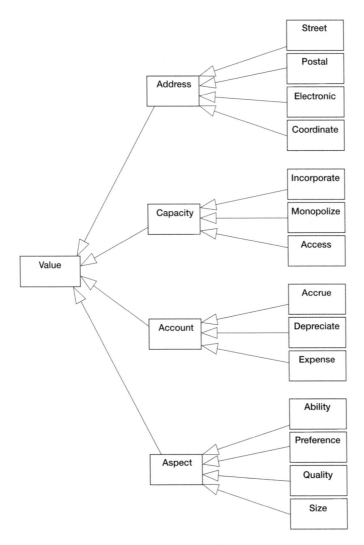

Figure 4-10 Entity Values

purchasing, manufacturing, design, and accounting—known as organization roles (see Organization Roles on page 140). An entity has an identity relative to each of its roles—an individual is identified as a person by name, as a taxpayer by Social Security number, as an employee by payroll number, as a student by a student code, and as a patient by some form of patient identity.

An identity identifies an entity in a context.

While an entity has a globally unique internal identity, it is accessible only by means of a name in a context, or an identifier, which is a name unique within the context. For example, a vehicle is uniquely identified by an asset number in an accounting context, by a registration number for licensing, and by a maintenance code for servicing. An identity is used to identify the specific entity instance with each business process instance by which it is affected. The definition of a business process typically specifies the kinds of entities with which it interacts, not specific instances. For example, a purchase order needs a supplier and one or more product line items, a financial journal references two or more ledger accounts, a payment is directed to a payee—each of these is a type, not an instance, of an entity. The specific entity instances are selected when a process instance is enacted, which requires the ability to locate suitable instances.

A business entity can be located in several ways.

An entity instance is typically located by its name or identity from a list of suitable candidates, either manually by an actor or automatically by selection rules applied in the context of the process. A key is an identity, sometimes called an accelerator, that uniquely identifies an entity for it to be located rapidly by means of an index. Part numbers, employee codes, personal identities, and ledger accounts are commonly used as keys. A partial key may be used to create a list of candidates from which the target is selected. An entity may also be selected by traversing a tree of increasingly specific names, which solves the "megadata" problem of searching one large dataset instead of many small sets [Sims 1994].

Selection criteria clip or filter the options.

Some intelligence is added to the selection process by specifying criteria that clip or filter the list or tree to reduce its size. By refining the selection criteria, the alternatives available to the user are progressively reduced until the selection is made. This approach is well suited to the selection of goods and services, where a consumer can specify preferences but is not able to identify a specific product. Many Internet shopping sites use known customer attributes to filter their product offerings. The tourism industry similarly maps vague desires to specific travel destinations, accommodations, and services, often requiring knowledge and expertise beyond that of a typical travel agent.

Intelligent software agents are well suited to this kind of task, using artificial intelligence techniques [Bigus and Bigus 1998]. The selection hierarchies described above become decision trees, which evaluate rules at each node. In particular, backward chaining enables a target entity to be located by means of a series of leading questions and answers. These so called "expert systems" emulate the behavior of human experts, progressively automating their work. Many business processes provide sufficient information for such an agent to select appropriate entities. For example, routing of work in production may be automated by selecting machines and tools according to their abilities, dimensions, and capacities.

Locate entities with intelligent agents.

Entity Roles

An entity is modeled by one or more roles, each of which represents it in a particular organizational and process context. Roles depend on how an enterprise is organized, and so vary between domains and companies. The "real" behavior of an entity is delegated to its values, which tend to be reusable both within and between domains. The primary justification of a role is that it controls complexity by partitioning knowledge of an entity into separate domains, and by allowing that knowledge to change over time. A role may be thought of as a facade by which to identify and locate an entity, and behind which to hide its values [D'Souza and Wills 1999]. The concepts are illustrated in this section by a typical, if short, selection of common entity roles.

Roles model an entity in different contexts.

Party

A party is an entity that does business with others, also known as a legal entity and involved party, typically an individual or an organization that has the capacity to enter into contracts. Examples in

A party is an entity that contracts with others.

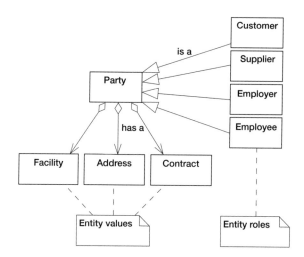

Figure 4-11 Party Roles and Values

business include customers and suppliers, employers and employ-ees, consultants and clients, taxpayers and collectors, and the pro-viders and receivers of services. It is no coincidence that these parties are coupled, because a contract often defines the relation-ship between two (or more) parties. For example, an employment contract defines the relationship between employer and employee, and a supply agreement involves both customer and supplier.

Different parties have similar values. Different parties have similar values: each has a set of addresses by which it may be located, accounts for recording financial transactions, and contracts for defining relationships with others. A receivable account records the financial transactions of a customer, whereas a payable account records those of a supplier. An employment con-tract defines the rights of the employee and the obligations of the employer, and vice versa. Each party uses addresses to communi-cate with others electronically, physically, and by post. Party is therefore an essential component of an enterprise model, some-times in its abstract form, but more often specialized to suit specific relationships.

Customer

A *customer* is a party to a contract in terms of which products are supplied, typically involving a supplier and other parties such as agents, shippers, insurers, and bankers. A contract empowers the customer to request delivery of goods and services under specified conditions, and in turn obliges the customer to pay for them within a specified time. Financial aspects are managed through a receivable account, which may be either unique to the customer or shared with others. For example, a company may have several depots, branches, or outlets in different locations, each of which is treated as a separate customer for delivery purposes. Credit control and collection of receivable amounts, however, might be done for the company as a whole by means of a shared receivable account. Other values record the personal details of key personnel, contact addresses, and specific pricing policies.

An entity may be a customer in an agreement.

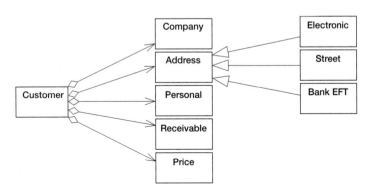

Figure 4-12   Customer Party

Employee

An employee is a party employed by another party—the employer—under terms and conditions defined in an employment contract. Each employee has his or her own personal details and, optionally, personal details of other family members. Street, postal, and electronic addresses at work and home are typically required, as are

Employment sets the conditions on which a person is employed.

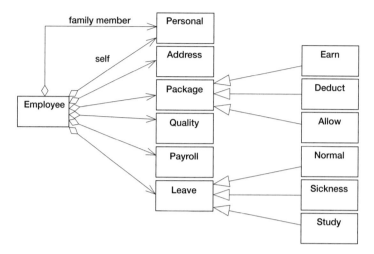

Figure 4-13   Employee Party

qualities from an employment perspective (education, skills, experience). The employee's remuneration package typically comprises a portfolio of earnings, allowances, and deductions. The payroll account records the accrual and payment of these earnings, as well as other financial transactions such as advances, loans, and repayments. Similar records of leave of absence may be required.

Actor

Actors initiate and activate process steps.

An actor is responsible for initiating processes and performing process steps initiated by other actors. Each actor is authorized to enact process instances from a list of process definitions—in effect, a menu of operations that it may start (see Figure 4-14).

An actor has one or more workflow roles.

Process types may be added and deleted, typically through an administrative process, to broaden or restrict the scope of an actor's responsibilities. Each actor is also assigned one or more organization roles, to which instances of individual process steps are allocated by process workflow. An actor may request work from a role when ready (pull allocation), or the role may send work to its actors according to scheduling rules (push allocation). Actors are

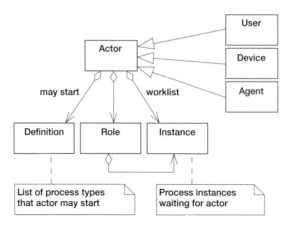

Figure 4-14 Actor Roles

usually human users, but may also include electronic devices and software agents. These topics are discussed more fully in the next chapter (see Organization Role on page 158).

Artifact

Artifacts are the things that are acted on by processes, and the artifact role of an entity models these passive or reactive aspects. Although artifacts are diverse, they tend to share certain kinds of values, such as their specifications, capacities, and costs. These values are particularly relevant to the artifacts used by processes, known as resources, for which capacity and cost are essential in many domains.The capacity of a resource includes its inventory, its ability to perform work, and its accessibility to business processes. Specifications range from simple descriptions to detailed lists of the qualities, abilities, and other aspects of the artifact. Costs are used to account for financial values of an artifact (see Figure 4-15).

Artifacts are the things used by processes.

Asset

An asset role models an entity that has capital expenditure, depreciation, and other such requirements. Dissimilar entities such as buildings, office equipment, production machines, vehicles, and

An entity can be a financial asset.

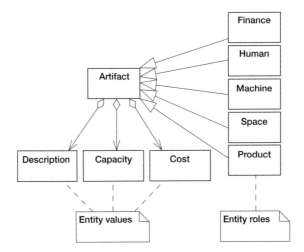

Figure 4-15   Artifact Roles and Values

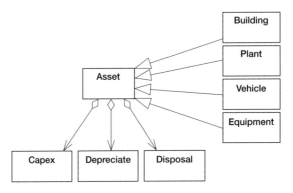

Figure 4-16   Asset Artifact

containers are financial assets, but share very few other characteristics. The role has one or more capital expenditure accounts against which initial costs are accrued, and for major refurbishments and improvements of the entity. It typically has one depreciation account, and often has two or more such accounts, with each one having different depreciation rates and policies for tax, management accounting, and replacement purposes.

Finance

The rather trivial example of an interest-bearing financial artifact having a facility illustrates some common concepts—the interest representing its cost and the facility representing its capacity. Other entity values might include an address for electronic funds transfer, an account for financial management and audit, and descriptions for marketing, administrative, and regulatory purposes. Although too simple a model from the banking or investment perspective, it may well be adequate for many operational purposes.

Financial artifacts may have capacity, price, and cost.

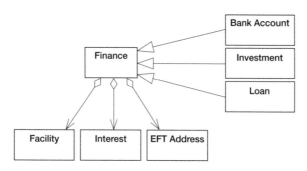

Figure 4-17 Finance Artifact

Human Resource

A human resource is a role of a person that is distinctly different from the role of actor. While an actor is responsible for initiating and controlling processes, a human resource models the productive abilities, capacities, and costs of people used in processes. Ability is typically used to select suitable candidates for the processes, capacity is used to schedule the work, and the payroll account is used to accrue earnings for piecework, attendance, and other remuneration schemes based on such operations. Capacity in the case of a human resource may also depend on leave commitments, which are detailed in yet another value.

Human resources model people's productive capacity.

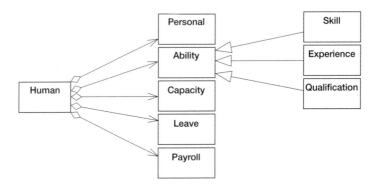

Figure 4-18 Human Resource

Machine Resource

Machines have abilities, capacities, and costs.

An entity has a machine role when it is used as a resource in a process, as opposed to when it is the product of a process (see Figure 4-19). In the second case, the entity is modeled by (surprise!) its product role. Machines are selected and scheduled according to their abilities and capacities in much the same way as human resources are selected and scheduled. Maintenance processes monopolize machine capacity just as any other process does, which differs in approach from leave taken by humans. Other values that are typical of machines are their costs, dimensions, and descriptive specifications.

Product

Products are traded, and may be made.

A product is an artifact that is bought and sold, including standard and configurable goods and services, both physical and intangible. Most products have marketing, operating, and service descriptions, and prices and costs. Intangible products include medical, legal, engineering, accounting, management, and other professional services; many types of agency; repair and maintenance; and sports and entertainment. Each of these products typically has a price or rate by which the service is charged, and is delivered by enacting a business process using people, vehicles, space, and other products. For example, a travel service requires vehicles and their crews, an

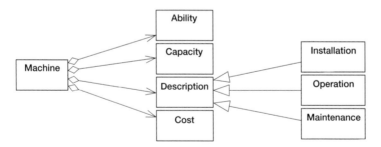

Figure 4-19   Machine Resource

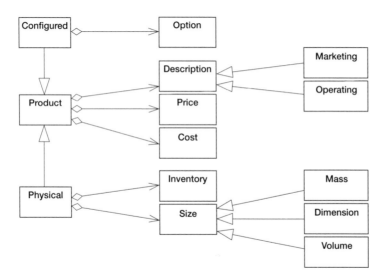

Figure 4-20   Product Artifacts

accommodation service needs buildings and rooms, and entertainment requires people and venues.

Most physical products are tangible entities offered for sale on a relatively continuous basis, often in a variety of package sizes. Foods and beverages, fuels and lubricants, household and commercial durables, and appliances and fittings are offered as standard products. Each typically has a unique Universal Product Code (UPC), a

Standard products are typically tangible entities.

price list, physical dimensions and mass with predefined shipping instructions and costs, and other standard features. Physical products are often held in manufacturing, distribution, and retail inventories to enable rapid supply of demand.

A configurable product has options.

A configurable product is one that has several options that are selected by a customer when the product is ordered. Typical examples include motor vehicles, personal computers, office furniture, travel and accommodation packages, and certain financial services. A particular configuration is determined by selecting appropriate options in a hierarchy, which manages dependencies among the options—a form of decision tree. Pricing of a configurable product is calculated on the basis of the options that have been selected, each of which has a standard price or cost.

Space, Place, and Location

A place is a space with a location.

A place where business is done, such as a country, city, factory, depot, building, or room, is modeled by its space role. A space typically has street, postal, and electronic addresses by which it is located, physical

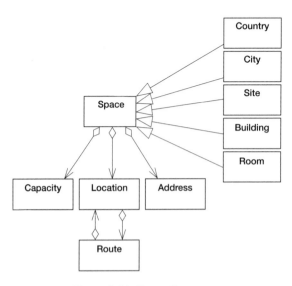

Figure 4-21 Space Resource

size to define its capacity, and a location for shipping, distributing, and other moving purposes. Although the concepts of space and location may be separated, most logistical business processes use both space and location in close combination. A location is of interest only if it can be reached from other locations by a route for which the mode of travel (road, rail, air, or water) and the length in distance and/or time are specified. This is of interest in transportation systems, supply chains, and facilities planning, and may be used on a smaller scale to route the flow of parts within a factory or of people within a building.

Entity Values

The preceding section illustrates that an entity can be modeled by a collection of properties comprising its roles, which identify it in various contexts, and its values, which are intrinsic to the entity. This section describes some commonly used entity values, including account, address, aspect, capacity, description, and price. Many other values are needed to build a comprehensive enterprise model. Relatively small-grained components such as these are useful, mainly because their meanings are well understood and because no advantage would be gained by changing them. Being reusable, they are good candidates for standardization within and between organizations and for implementation as business and software components.

Values model the intrinsic properties of an entity.

Account

An account measures the financial value of an entity, modeled by a subaccount in a financial ledger or by a property of the entity (see Financial Ledger on page 38). Centralized accounting favors the ledger approach, whereas a decentralized approach favors the account values described in this section. Figure 4-22 shows an account in which a list of open items records values posted as a result of process steps acting on an entity, and a list of accounting periods references items that occurred during each period. An item records the process that created it and the financial value with

An account measures the financial value of an entity.

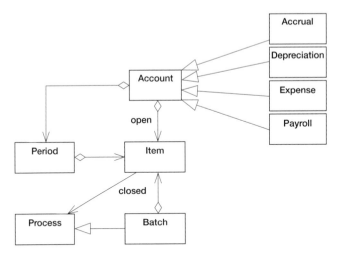

Figure 4-22   Account Values

which the account is debited or credited. Open items are periodically reconciled and batched by matching processes, thereby moving them from open to closed status.

Sequence of actions to post to an account. Figure 4-23 illustrates the sequence of actions that occur during posting from a business process to an account, which is a value of an
entity used by the process. The account accesses the period during
which the process occurs, if it exists, and otherwise creates and
appends a new period (typically using an accounting calendar to determine period dates). The period then gets the item for the process, if it
exists, and otherwise creates a new item. The financial value of the
item is incremented by the posted amount, and it is appended to both
the period item list and the account open item list. This ensures that
there is only one item per account per process step, which is required
to post multiple entries to the same account within a single step.

Financial trans-actions may be matched. Financial transactions have a duality by which they may be
matched [McCarthy 1982]. For example, invoices may be matched
to payments received from customers, accrued tax is matched to
payments made to the Internal Revenue Service, and bank account

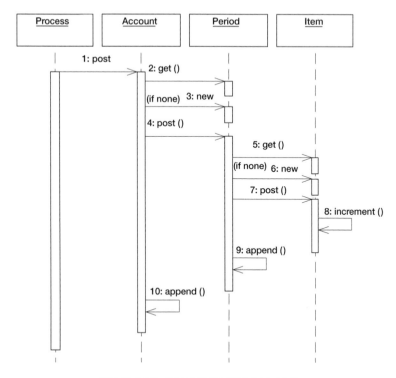

Figure 4-23   Account Posting Sequence

transactions are matched when reconciling balances. A batch process matches the open items of an account according to rules that
depend on the type of account. Most require that the total value of
the items in a batch be zero, so that the sum of the value of open
items equals the balance of the account. If matched, the selected
items are removed from the account's list of open items; otherwise,
they are removed from the batch. Various types of account are
derived from this generic account to add the behavior required
under specific circumstances. Some of these accounts are described
in the following subsections.

Accrual Account

An accrual account is used when there is a difference between the
time when a financial transaction is recognized and the time when

*Accrual accounts cater
to timing differences.*

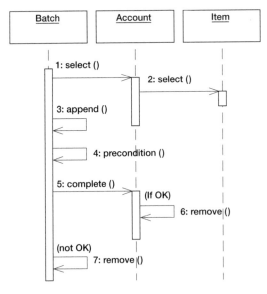

Figure 4-24 Account Matching

it is settled. For example, sales, purchase, and income taxes are accrued when a sale, purchase, or payroll transaction occurs, but the tax authority is paid the accrued amount at a later date. The value of a purchase may be accrued between receipt and invoice, the cost of work in process may be accrued until complete, interest on a loan may be accrued until paid, and so on. A variant of an accrual account, known as a control account, controls the values of entities that should remain substantially unchanged over time. Accounts payable and accounts receivable are well-known examples of such accounts.

Cost Account

Cost accounts model different aspects for various purposes.

A cost account implements the business rules for establishing the cost of an entity, including standard, average, actual, and latest costs. Entities may have multiple costs to reflect different aspects (such as material, labor, and burden) and for different purposes (such as standard for accounting, latest for pricing). Cost accounts specialize generic accounts to include the attributes and operations required to calculate and record such costs. Standard cost accounts, for example, might record variances between standard and actual costs of inventory, machine and human resources, and in-project activities. Cost accounts are widely used in manufacturing, project, and distribution environments.

Depreciation Account

Depreciation accounts extend the generic account to include policies and rates, and the initial, depreciated, revaluation, and disposal costs required for depreciation calculations. These accounts calculate and record the accumulated depreciation value of an entity, including the initial depreciation allowance. Depreciation may be calculated according to straight-line, reducing-balance, or other rules. Other operations enable an asset to be revalued, and to record the profit or loss on disposal.

Policies and rates for calculating depreciation.

Expense Account

Many entities that are used or consumed in business processes do not warrant detailed modeling, but their cost or revenue is sufficient for budgeting and recording in financial terms. Examples include consumables in manufacturing, stationery in offices, rent and utility costs in buildings, tires and lubricants for vehicles, and sales of scrap materials and by-products. An expense account is budgeted according to various policies and is updated by actual values in the same way a generic account is updated. Budget values may be based on previous values, may be determined by splitting a single value across multiple periods, or may be based on relationships to other budget, planned, or forecast values (see Financial Ledger on page 38).

A simple entity model is an expense account.

Tax Account

A tax account is a special kind of accrual account for calculating and accruing tax values and for applying the appropriate payment policies. Value added and sales taxes are typically quite simple, but may depend on categories of sale or purchase and on the jurisdiction.

Tax accounts accrue and pay taxes.

Income taxes for individuals and companies are rather more complex but are readily modeled by tables or algorithms. Most other taxes tend to be specialized and are applicable to relatively few entities.

Address

An address locates an entity.

An address is used to locate an entity, including its physical, postal, and electronic addresses and its phone and fax numbers. The concept of address is navigational: a street address locates by street, a room address locates within a building or complex, a postal address is used by postal services to deliver to the addressee, an e-mail address locates by means of the Internet, and an electronic funds transfer (EFT) address locates a bank account to deliver messages through network services. Phone and fax numbers are also addresses, because they are used to locate the called party using a telephone system.

Coordinate Address

Coordinate addresses locate geographically.

A coordinate address locates an entity relative to a coordinate system, which is typically, but not necessarily, geographical. It enables an entity to determine its location and the distances and directions to other addressable entities. Coordinates for particular purposes include latitude and longitude, map references, building floor and room number, seat row and number, and many other schemes that can be interpreted to find the addressed entity.

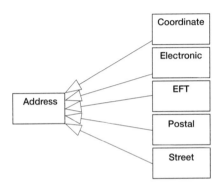

Figure 4-25 Address Values

Electronic Address

An electronic address enables an entity to be located by means of public, cellular, and other phone systems, value added network services, the Internet, and other electronic communications facilities. The electronic address of an entity might therefore include phone, fax, and cellphone numbers, e-mail address, and World Wide Web site URL. Other attributes might include EDI, EFT, and other electronic message addresses. Electronic funds transfer (EFT) requires such an address to locate the bank account or other financial entity to and from which money is transferred. An EFT address may differ for domestic versus international transfers, but typically is highly standardized. Typical EFT address attributes include a bank number, branch number, and account type, number, and name. Additional attributes for international transfers might include the bank and branch names, the country, city, and postal code, and a contact phone number for queries.

Electronic addresses locate by means of communications networks.

Postal Address

A postal address locates an entity through the global postal system, and occasionally by means of military or private postal services. It differs from a street address when the addressed entity has a post office box or bag, and when it has a mailroom separate from its physical location. The attributes of a postal address typically include the post office box or bag number, the post office, the state or province, the country, and the postal code. Postal addresses of mobile entities, such as in the military and project environments, may have organizational attributes.

A postal address locates an entity through a postal system.

Street Address

A street address is a form of coordinate address for physically locating an entity, typically for transport and travel purposes. Its attributes typically include street name and number, suburb, estate or area, city or town, state or province, country, and postal code. The address may be extended to include, for example, the building name, floor, and room number. The attributes of a street address

A street address is used for physically locating an entity.

are often used to group entities that are in close proximity for marketing and transport purposes.

Aspect

An entity has many other aspects—indeed the word "aspect" might be applied to any of its properties or attributes. In this context, however, an aspect is a catchall for properties that are not otherwise modeled. A few examples will now be presented to illustrate how knowledge of an entity may be enhanced through aspects such as its abilities, preferences, qualities, and size (Figure 4-26).

Ability

An entity may have several abilities.

Most entities are usable in several ways, each of which is an ability. A power tool may be able to drill, cut, sand, and polish, depending on its attachments; a person may be able to analyze, design, program, and manage software projects; and a vehicle may be able to transport free-flowing products including liquids, grains, and pellets. Each is a set of abilities that may be useful in a business (or other) context. Indeed, the main purpose of this value is to enable suitable entities to be selected for business processes that require specific abilities.

Preference

An entity has preferences that affect its value and behavior.

An entity, particularly a person, may have preferences that influence its value, behavior, and effectiveness. Preferences are of particular interest in marketing processes, where factors such as residence,

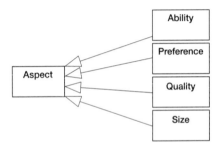

Figure 4-26 Aspects of an Entity

travel, entertainment, sport, recreation, dining, pricing, and other such preferences are used to target consumers. The concept may be extended to model operating conditions for machines, procurement habits of companies, remuneration preferences of employees, and so on.

Quality

The quality of an entity also affects its value—such as the profession, qualifications, experience, and skills of a person; the portability, scalability, reliability, flexibility, durability, and efficiency of a software system; or the beauty, accessibility, and diversity of a location—often qualities that are intangible and abstract. Qualities tend to be subjective and difficult to quantify, but are important if the full value of an entity is to be modeled. Enumerated lists of options are often the best way in which to represent qualities, typically weighted according to the needs of a particular process or role.

The quality of an entity also affects its value.

Size

The size of an entity might include its useful dimensions (such as length, height, width, thickness, and depth), its mass and volume, and other more specialized quantities [Fowler 1997]. Such aspects must include their units of measure, which typically enable conversion to quantities in equivalent units. Physical size is important for entities engaged in logistical processes such as manufacturing, distribution, construction, and maintenance. Other sizes and quantities are needed in particular roles, depending on the needs of the processes with which they are involved.

The size of an entity includes its useful dimensions.

Capacity

Capacity models the ability of an entity to be used in a business process, such as inventory for making products, money for purchasing materials, credit for selling to customers, and human and machine time for performing tasks. Taylor proposes four basic types of capacity, which depend on how the capacity is acquired at the start, and how it is released at the end, of a process [Taylor 1995].

Entity capacity is used by business processes.

Type	Behavior	Example
Consume	Ceases to have separate identity	Chemical in a reaction
Incorporate	Keeps its identity in a composite entity	Part in an assembly
Monopolize	Not available to others while in use	Machine during a cycle
Access	Available to others while in use	Information about a process

Process steps acquire and release entities.

The simple production process shown in Figure 4-27 illustrates in four steps how capacity is used, released, and created. The first step accesses information and issues raw material and components to the process. The information is returned immediately, having been accessed but not consumed. A pallet and a machine are acquired in the second step, the machine being released in the subsequent step but the pallet remaining in use until the fourth step. The product is also released from the process in the fourth step, becoming available for storage, transport, or use.

Capacity is consumed, monopolized, or accessed.

Capacity that is consumed or incorporated is permanently lost when used, monopolized capacity is not available to others for the duration of the process, and accessed capacity is available except perhaps for a brief moment during access. Figure 4-28 illustrates

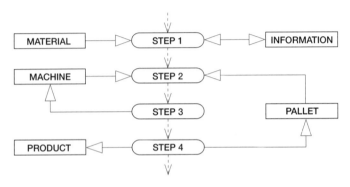

Figure 4-27 Process and Capacity

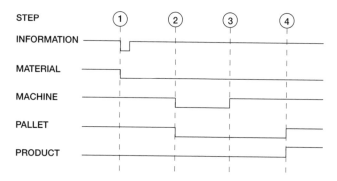

Figure 4-28 Capacity Timing Diagram

how each kind of capacity is used and released before, during, and after a process step. The capacity is available for use by other processes at all other times, and scheduling processes balance the demand for, and supply of, capacity to maximize its utilization and value. Typically, demand processes are aggregated into cycles, each of which has a single supply process. There may be more than one supply process per cycle if demand patterns change rapidly, or if other constraints dictate multiple processes (for example, a maximum delivery quantity may dictate multiple deliveries).

Firm demand processes are scheduled for a number of cycles into the future, which is called the demand horizon. Demand is thereafter forecast for each cycle out to the forecast horizon (Figure 4-29). The duration of each planning cycle is usually, but not necessarily, the same as a scheduling cycle. For example, demand might be scheduled for six weeks into the future, and planning might be done for twelve months. Dependent demand is calculated from the source of its demand where this is possible: demand for a component part or material can be calculated from that of its parent product by using a bill of material; payment due to a supplier is planned from the receipt of goods and services, with knowledge of the applicable payment terms.

Capacity is planned and used in cycles.

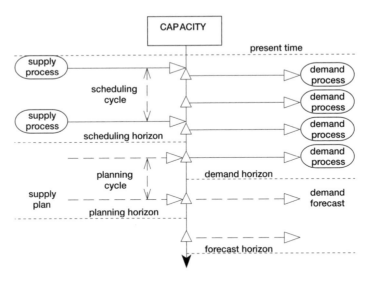

Figure 4-29   Scheduling Capacity

Consumed and Incorporated Capacity

Inventory and money are accumulated.

Physical inventory, bank accounts and cash, receivable and payable accounts, and many natural resources have capacities that do not depend on the flow of time but on the cumulative effect of supply and demand. The capacity or balance is increased by a supply process and decreased by each demand process. Scheduled capacity may also be increased by planned processes and decreased by forecast demand. Material requirements planning uses this to initiate manufacturing and purchase processes to meet demand; financial managers use it to predict cash flow and decide how much and when to pay.

Monopolized Capacity

Monopolized capacity depends on available time.

Human and machine resources have capacities that depend on the time that they are available to do work. When in use by a process, they are monopolized and their capacity is not available for other work. When the process ends, their capacity again becomes available. This kind of capacity depends on working time, which may not be available at night, on weekends or holidays, or during leave periods. The time available (or not available) is usually defined by a scheduling calendar, which may apply to a single capacity or, more typically, to many.

Accessed Capacity

Some entities have either zero or infinite capacity; quite simply, they are either available or not available. Electronic drawings and specifications may be used concurrently by an unlimited number of processes; the capacity of a specialized tool is unimportant if it is used on only one product; a view may be appreciated by all in good weather during the day, but by none at night. Capacity of this type may be thought of as having a Boolean schedule, being either available or not available at a particular time. For example, a drawing is available between the time when it is approved and the time when it is superseded, a tool is available except when it is being manufactured or serviced, and the sun shines between sunrise and sunset.

Some entities have either zero or infinite capacity.

Description

An entity may be described in many ways, very often by simple linear text, but many business situations benefit from standardized and organized data that can be used systematically. Descriptions may have graphical and structural representations, some of which are widely used and in predefined formats. The means by which entities are modeled will become richer as multimedia and other technologies extend the descriptive power available to users. Certain types of information are regulated by law, or have been established by convention, to the extent that they are practically standardized. Examples include company and personal details, product structures, and various types of specifications and drawings.

An entity has textual, graphical, and structural descriptions.

Textual Description

Text remains a most flexible and effective means by which to describe an entity—or, for that matter, anything else. Textual information may be structured and tagged using XML (or other markup languages) to format it, to enhance its semantic value, and to

Text is a good way to describe things.

improve its readability by machines. The main disadvantage of text is that it is in a particular language, often with domain-specific terminology and jargon that is not well understood by others. However, textual descriptions are likely to survive for some considerable time to come.

Graphical Description

Graphical descriptions help to convey meaning.

The old adage that a picture is worth a thousand words may be challenged, but graphical descriptions can certainly help to convey meaning. The UML diagrams in this book supplement its textual content with graphical descriptions. Graphics is typically vector based—as in drawings and diagrams—or in a multitude of static and dynamic pictorial formats. Drawings are widely used to describe products, machines, buildings, and other physical artifacts. Pictures describe products, people, locations, and other visually important entities.

Structural Description

Structure describes how an entity is formed or assembled.

The structure of an entity is important for many reasons, particularly if the entity is to be created or assembled from other entities. For example, a product structure describes the components of a product or assembly, which may differ for purchasing, production, maintenance, and logistical purposes. The shape of an entity may also be described through the structure of its elements, as used in finite element analysis. Product data management standards for describing and exchanging such information are now emerging [ISO 10303 1994].

Company Description

Business details are for legal and financial purposes.

Textual descriptions may be extended to include attributes that satisfy specific needs. Business requires the interaction of financial, commercial, industrial, and other kinds of companies. The description of such an entity typically includes its common name, legal name, registration number and date, tax number(s), and the nature of its business. These attributes are required for statutory and regulatory purposes and for unique identification of the company in legal and business contexts. The value is often used in contracts and legal and financial transactions.

Personal Description

Business also involves people in many roles and situations for which information is required. Personal details include the first, middle, and last names, sex, marital status, birth date, nationality, domicile, and identity and/or passport numbers. These attributes are used primarily in processes that need sympathetic contact—with consumers, employees, family members, or personnel in other organizations—where such information is used to personalize the relationship. Note that in certain jurisdictions some of this information may not be acquired or used, for reasons of privacy.

Personal details enable personalized contact.

Inventory

The inventory property maintains the quantity and composition of the stock of an entity, usually a physical product, but also of other physical assets. The simplest form is aggregate inventory, which records the on-hand (and perhaps the on-hold, or quarantine) quantity and cost of the entity, through methods by which it is received and issued. The lot property does this for each lot or batch

Inventory maintains the quantity of stock.

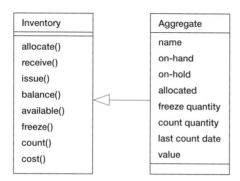

Figure 4-30   Inventory Value

of inventory that is received, usually issuing it in the same sequence as that in which it was received [first-in, first-out (FIFO) policy]. An integral lot inventory does not permit the splitting of lots on issue, which is typical of the textile, steel, cable, chemical, and other industries where products are supplied in rolls, bobbins, or drums that cannot be divided with ease. Serial lots identify each batch by a serial number or code, and serial items create a new lot for each individual item. The inventory property models only one aspect, with costs being modeled by cost accounts and time-phased availability being modeled by capacity.

Aggregate Inventory

Inventory is used in materials management.

To aggregate inventory, add quantities received to the on-hand balance, and subtract issues. The average cost can be calculated if the value of receipts is also aggregated. Inventory is allocated to reduce the available balance (on-hand—allocated) for simple materials planning. Should inventory not be available for use, record it as being on hold until such time as it may be used, when it is on-hand. Inventory is periodically counted for audit purposes, but it is often not feasible to suspend transactions while the count is being made. The inventory balance is recorded at the time of the count, and this

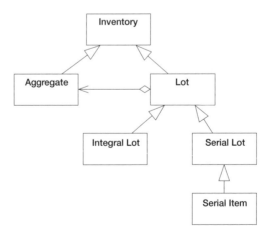

Figure 4-31 Inventory Options

freeze quantity is compared with the actual count quantity. The difference between the quantities is applied to the on-hand quantity when the count is finalized, thereby enabling transactions to continue in the interim. Note that these operations are shared by all inventory subtypes.

Inventory Lots

This property is used when each receipt of inventory is to be separately recorded—typically, to ensure stock rotation and to record individual costs. On receipt of a lot, an aggregate inventory property is created for it, and is added at the end of a list. Issues are from lots at the start of the list to ensure that the oldest inventory is used first, and if the lot then has zero balance, it is deleted. The on-hand, on-hold and allocated quantities of the inventory are calculated by summing the equivalent quantities of each lot. Similar approaches are used to determine the cost of the inventory and to freeze and count its quantities.

A lot is an aggregate inventory for each receipt.

Integral Lots

An integral lot is similar to the inventory lot described above, except that it can be issued only as a whole, or integral, lot. This is typical of situations where an entity is packaged in such a way that it cannot be split or divided for issue. The whole lot is issued, and any surplus is received again as a new lot of lesser size. For example, a drum of cable might be issued whole and then be received back minus the quantity of cable that has been used. Other examples include rolls of fabric, paper, and plastic; reels of sheet, strip, and wire; tanks of fuel, oils, paints, and chemicals; and containers of predetermined, fixed quantities.

An integral lot can only be issued whole.

Serial Lots

A serial lot is also similar to an inventory lot but requires that the lot number be specified on receipt, and optionally on issue, of the inventory. Inventory is serialized for quality assurance purposes to enable items to be tracked in a value chain. Serial codes are mandated

A serial lot is identified by its serial number or code.

in some industries—pharmaceuticals, for example—and are used for convenience in many others. A serial code may be a description in certain situations, such as in the case of textiles, which must be from the same batch in order to be used in the same set of clothing.

Serial Items

A serial item is a serial inventory lot of one.

A serial item is a serial inventory lot of one entity, each of which has its own serial identification. The serial code is captured or created on receipt of an item, and is referenced on its issue for use. Most entities of any significant value or operational significance have individual serial codes, which are sometimes used to identify the entities. Household appliances are identified in this way for warranty purposes; key automotive, electronic, and aerospace parts have serial codes for quality and maintenance tracking; and large, complex engineering entities are serialized for configuration management. By classifying a serial item as inventory, it behaves in a business process as other inventories behave.

Price

Many kinds of entities are priced.

Price is a property of products (goods and services) that is also applied to finance, to assets, and to human, machine, and other resources. Simple prices are fixed per unit of the entity that is being priced, and are frequently effective for a range of dates. More complex

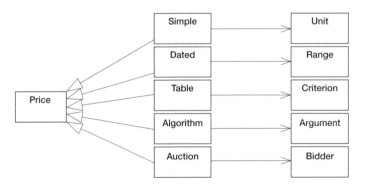

Figure 4-32 Price Options

situations are handled by tables in which prices depend on various criteria such as purchase quantity, delivery location, type of purchaser, means of payment, and so on. A price may also be calculated using an algorithm having one or more arguments, such as a markup or gross profit on cost. An ancient form of pricing that is now gaining favor over the Internet is auction, in which a price is reached by bidders in competition.

Simple Price

A simple price is a numeric value expressed per unit, which is multiplied by a quantity in that unit to determine the purchase or sales value of the entity. A simple price can be converted to another unit by a conversion factor, if available. This form of pricing is typical of standard products in stable situations where it is feasible to change the price explicitly when needed, and when such changes take immediate effect.

A simple price is a numeric value expressed per unit.

Dated Price

Prices typically change over time in response to market forces, seasons, inflation or deflation, exchange rate volatility, product obsolescence, and many other factors. Such a price is valid for only specified dates, and a date must be specified in order to determine the ruling price. This kind of pricing is used where orders are taken and deliveries made at different times, and where regular price changes occur but other factors are stable. A dated price also enables price trends and cycles to be analyzed and perhaps projected.

A dated price is valid for only specified dates.

Price Table

Price tables are used where price is affected simultaneously by several criteria—and a list of the values of those criteria must be specified to determine the ruling price. A table typically has a dimension or axis for each criterion and has coordinates on each axis for the values that the criterion can have. Numeric criteria may also allow interpolation of prices for values that fall between coordinates. Time is usually one of the criteria, making the price table a generalization

A price table has an axis for each criterion.

of the dated price described above. Other criteria might include entity aspects, entity locations, and process types.

Pricing Algorithm

Pricing algorithms calculate prices from arguments.

Pricing algorithms range from calculations of markup or gross profit on cost to sophisticated estimating and quotation programs often found in jobbing and project environments. However, all are able to determine a price from a set of one or more arguments, and so may be modeled independently of other entity values. Pricing algorithms may be based on some underlying theory or code, but are often merely rules of thumb that have been reduced to a set of formulas. The rationale behind such rules is sometimes difficult to comprehend, but the results are frequently useful.

Auction Price

An auction is the surest way of determining market value.

Pricing by auction is the surest way of determining market value at a particular place and time. Bidders compete on price in a marketplace for a specific entity, and the "best" price is accepted (or not) by the seller of the entity. This requires that the bid prices, and the parties making the bids, be recorded. The bids are typically evaluated and awarded after a predefined closing time or date, but may be closed when a predefined price is reached. Pricing of this nature is likely to become widespread as virtual organizations evolve (see Network Organization on page 145).

Summary

Entities are the physical and conceptual things that encapsulate much of the information about an enterprise, all of which is relative to particular points of view. Partitioning this knowledge by role has several benefits: each business domain is logically separated, a process step typically affects only one role of an entity, and roles can be added and removed as the processes in which the entity is involved change over time.

Values model the intrinsic shared properties of an entity, tending to be relatively simple attributes. They have the potential to be standardized, which helps communicate such information among disparate systems. Even without such standards, many values are reusable from entity to entity within an organization.

Modeling entities in this way runs the risk of creating stovepipe systems in which different aspects of the same entity are not related. This is avoided by ensuring that each entity has an internal identity that is recognized by, and that enables navigation and mapping among, all its properties. Each role identifies the entity in a context, and so the same entity may be accessed by different names or identities relative to each context.

Entity roles are reusable from process to process within an enterprise or business domain, while entity values are reusable between roles and domains. This enables complex things to be modeled by a set of relatively simple properties that can be added and deleted dynamically. Role properties should be standardized within an organization, and value properties are good candidates for global standardization.

5

Organization

Organization controls complexity by dividing an enterprise into manageable units and roles. Business processes flow both within and between organizations. The study of complexity indicates that traditional command and control of such processes will be replaced by systems of communication and coordination. An organization also provides a framework for modeling and managing its purpose, processes, and entities.

Organizations, Systems, and Complexity

Organizations have become the dominant form of institution in our society, and they impact almost all aspects of our lives. Most business is conducted by commercial organizations; we are governed by local, regional, national, and global organizations; and our education, health, welfare, and security are provided by diverse kinds of service organizations. We choose clubs and societies for our recreation, Internet bulletin boards and lists for our enlightenment, and communities in which to live. Organizations have traditionally been strongly influenced by location, but are now adapting to ubiquitous networks that remove geographic constraints. The virtual corporation is one such development.

Organizations are the dominant form of institution in society.

"An organization is a consciously coordinated social entity, with a relatively identifiable boundary, that functions on a relatively continuous basis to achieve a common goal or set of goals" [Robbins 1990].

Are organizations rational, goal-directed entities?

"An organization structure is a defined set of role relationships which, implicitly or explicitly, set limits of behavior and action and, hence, imply freedom of behavior within those limits. Remaining

Or power-based, political structures?

within those limits ensures tranquil role interactions; conflict comes from pushing beyond the limits" [Howard 1996].

Ambiguity sur-
rounds organiza-
tional theory.

These two very different definitions of organization illustrate the ambiguity that permeates organizational theory, particularly now that many of the assumptions on which it is based are being brought into question by technology. The first definition is of a rational organization whose purpose is clearly defined and sup-ported by its management. The second defines a social organization whose purpose is directed toward the individuals of which it is comprised. In reality, an organization has both rational and social aspects that influence its behavior.

Organization History

Organizations reflect
changes in the
environment.

Although the Roman army and the Catholic church introduced formal organization many centuries ago, it was not part of everyday life until the Industrial Revolution. Since that time, organizational thinking has evolved from closed to open systems and between rational and political behavior [Robbins 1990]. The modern enter-prise is an open system that engages in business processes as much between as within organizations, and that focuses on rational goals in order to survive and grow. Such organizations also recognize the freedom of individuals to learn, to move, and to influence and adapt their work practices. The inward-looking and coercive com-mand and control structures of the past hold little attraction for people in the new world economy, and are being replaced by coop-erative and open forms of management.

The job is being
replaced by the role.

Two centuries after modern industrial man created the idea of a job, new types of organization based on the concept of role are evolving. Careers in real and virtual organizations are shaped by alliances, ventures, and projects, not by a sequence of employment positions. Even within conventional corporations, the focus is increasingly on flexible abilities rather than on fixed positions. This has a major impact on their management and information systems.

Organizations of the Future

The Sloan School of Management at MIT has an initiative to explore the direction in which organizations will evolve into the twenty-first century [Laubacher et al. 1997]. One scenario envisions networks of small firms that form to address specific projects and disband when these projects are completed. They depend on a high-bandwidth, global electronic network to market, communicate, and deliver products and services. Autonomous units of one to ten people will respond to requests for their services in an open, network-based marketplace, with no need for centralized structures. Authority will be exercised through the allocation of capital to development, production, and marketing projects.

Networks of small firms form to address specific projects.

The concept of a job, together with health insurance and pension benefits, professional development and career path, and a sense of belonging, all but disappears in this scenario. The benefits of independence and flexible work are bought at the cost of insecurity, isolation, and loneliness. It is suggested that these issues might be resolved by other forms of organization similar to the guilds of the Middle Ages [Laubacher and Malone 1997]. A modern-day precedent is the Screen Actor's Guild, which provides health and pension benefits to its members in an industry where there is no security of ongoing employment. Other examples include alumni groups, neighborhood and regional organizations, families, and personal networks, each of which may provide some of the functions traditionally expected of an employer.

Independence and flexible work cause insecurity and loneliness.

A second scenario postulates that the world will be dominated by a few global conglomerates that will provide cradle-to-grave care for their employees. Many of the benefits currently provided by social democracies will be taken over by these large corporations. Through their pension and health insurance plans, employees will own a major share in the equity of such enterprises, and so will be able to have a significant influence on their management. Authority and decision making will be structured into a formal hierarchy, which

Will the world be dominated by global conglomerates?

will be populated by managers elected in much the same way that politicians are elected today. Employees will take their identity from and owe their loyalty to the employer rather than a nation, ethnic group, or family.

Networks of autonomous units emulate natural systems.

These two scenarios represent extremes in a spectrum of possibilities, and it is likely that reality will have aspects of each. However, the concept of networks of autonomous units that cooperate to achieve common purpose is closest to the behavior observed in natural systems. Geese flying in V formation are not directed by a lead bird, but merely use simple relative positioning to benefit from slipstream. Similarly, colonies of ants and swarms of bees achieve amazing feats without any centralized command structure, relying instead on various forms of communication to direct their purpose. A world with several billion more people than today is likely to tend toward this kind of swarm behavior.

Lower transaction costs will favor simpler organizations.

The scenario of networks of small groups seems likely for the conduct of operations. Large conglomerates will doubtlessly exist, mainly to accumulate and allocate capital. They themselves will increasingly rely on network technology to inform themselves in the global marketplace and to deploy their resources rapidly and effectively. Hierarchical management and information systems of command and control will be replaced by networks of small, largely autonomous units. Reducing transaction costs will favor many simpler organizations, supported by networks, over a few suppliers with large, monolithic systems. They will interact on a "peer-to-peer" basis with other such units to communicate and coordinate their work. This is perhaps the only way in which the exploding complexity of modern business will be manageable.

Organization Units

Organizations are systems.

A system is "an abstract idea of a whole having emergent properties, a layered structure and processes of communication and control which in principle enable it to survive in a changing environment"

[Checkland 1981]. Checkland's definition of a system is the same as our definition of an organization unit. Organization units group entities and processes that are tightly coupled, while minimizing their dependency on others. For example, a body has a heart, lungs, a liver, and other organs that operate largely independently of each other but are coupled by the nervous system and a network of blood vessels. A company similarly has autonomous departments for purchasing, sales, accounting, and manufacturing that are connected by a logistical system and an information network by which the company performs its work.

The central theme of organization is management, and each organization unit is responsible for the management of its purpose, processes, and entities. The static purpose of a unit is defined by policies and contracts detailing the work it can do, the conditions under which the work is done, and the courses of action that are taken when the policies and contracts are violated. A unit is obliged to perform the work requested by any other unit that fulfills these conditions. The dynamic purpose of the unit is the schedule of obligations, or *agenda*, incurred in terms of the policies and contracts. Business processes are instantiated to fulfill the obligations, and entities are allocated to the processes (see Organizations on page 20). An organization unit therefore has a number of specific management responsibilities, typically implemented by a set of managers.

Management is the central theme of organization.

A purpose or contract manager is responsible for the policies, contracts, schedules, and budgets of the organization—ensuring its proper direction. A process manager uses workflow, transaction, and security services to enact, direct, and execute business processes correctly. An entity manager selects suitable entities according to criteria supplied by each process. A unit also manages communications with other units. Incoming messages are interpreted according to the intent of the sender to query, direct, assert, and otherwise influence the unit. Outgoing messages are directed

Responsibilities are undertaken by managers.

to known addresses or subscribers or facilitators, or are broadcast. The style of management dictates the relative autonomy that the unit has over its affairs, and how much it is influenced by others.

A unit is a distinct, identifiable object.

Finally, an organization unit is at a higher level of abstraction than its component objects, and is itself a distinct, identifiable object. Each unit has one or more addresses by which it is located by other units using the available electronic, postal, and transport services. As a subsidiary of another, a unit is modeled as an entity in the parent unit, which, being recursive, allows organization hierarchies of unlimited depth. However, for reasons outlined later in this chapter, it may not be desirable to model complex organizations in this way.

Organization Roles

A viewpoint helps to manage complexity.

Decomposition of an organization into a set of autonomous, interacting units is necessary, but not sufficient, to manage its full complexity. For further partitioning of units, each unit is modeled from several different business points of view, or organization roles. Each role is a perspective in a frame of reference, and at a level of abstraction, from which to view the organization. Typical roles, which often have names ending in the suffix "-ing," are as follows [Ould 1995]:

- Accounting: accounting and financial aspects

- Engineering: for design, specification, and configuration

- Maintaining: service, repair, and maintenance aspects

- Managing: command, control, and coordination aspects

- Manufacturing: relating to physical production

- Marketing: customer needs and preferences

- Planning: view into the future

- Quality: for conformance to specification

- Shipping: transportation and distribution aspects

- Supporting: relating to use by customers

Each role is a viewpoint from which the appropriate *subject matter experts* can define business requirements. For example, a product might be separately modeled from the accounting, engineering, maintenance, manufacturing, quality, and shipping points of view. A single business process might similarly involve marketing, planning, manufacturing, and accounting roles.

An entity is modeled by a set of role properties (see Entity Roles on page 103), each of which defines its behavior in the context of an organization role. The engineering role of a product might use its indented bill of material, the purchasing role the summary bill, and the production role its manufacturing bill. These in turn might be modeled by a single integrated bill, or might use separate bills, depending on design and implementation decisions. The role has merely defined what is required in a particular context, not how it is to be implemented.

An entity is modeled from several points of view.

A role activity diagram is similarly used to partition the steps of a business process between organization roles (see Role Activity Diagram on page 69). A process step thus interacts with entities by means of appropriate roles, each in the same organization context. Purpose is also defined and measured for each role (see Measures of Purpose on page 31), enabling a suitable measure of the process step. Mechanical and human actors are also classified according to their roles, which in turn determine the processes that they can perform and the information that they can access.

Process steps are partitioned between roles.

The idea that roles help to manage complexity by partitioning the problem into different *areas of concern*, each of which is handled independently, is a well-established modeling principle. RM-ODP, the OORAM software engineering method, and the OMG's business object component architecture each use viewpoints or roles for this

Organization roles help manage complexity.

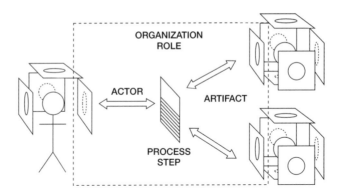

Figure 5-1   Actor, Process, and Artifact

purpose [Reenskaug 1996]. The roles described in this section enable selective "projections" by which to model an organization. Figure 5-1 illustrates an actor operating on two artifacts in a single process step, each having the same organization role.

Complexity is also controlled by levels of abstraction.

A model is also partitioned by level of abstraction. Complexity between one level and the next is not linear, but can increase by one or two orders of magnitude. While difficult to justify, this claim is supported by observations of organizational structure and behavior [Robbins 1990]. An empirical guideline for defining the granularity of levels of abstraction and organization roles is Taylor's principle of "nested nine's," which states that a view in any particular context should not have more than nine key concepts [Taylor 1995]. Levels form a hierarchical structure to partition the organization for this purpose.

Organization Structure

Information on the organization of an enterprise is used in many ways.

An organizational structure "includes information about the organizational units that make up a company (or organization), the human resources that belong to those organizational units, as well as the structure and relationships that connect them all together" [OMG 1998]. Information about the organization of an enterprise and its employees is required for workflow, security, payroll, taxation, budgeting, and accounting reasons. An organizational hierarchy also defines the power relationship between units that establishes obligations and commitments to each other, enabling the coordination of distributed work [Dignum and Weigand 1994].

Hierarchical Organization

An enterprise of any significant size requires broad strategic and tactical planning capabilities, and a rich set of efficient transactions [OMG 1997]. While operational transactions such as sales, purchases, and payments are well understood, transactions are rarely extended to tactical and strategic levels. Strategic plans and budgets may also be propagated, and management information reported, throughout an enterprise according to its organization. However, this is often hampered by the hierarchical structure of organizations, as illustrated by the theoretical and desired paths of communication shown in Figure 5-2.

Organizations are horizontally and vertically integrated.

An enterprise is typically organized along several dimensions, including:

- Vertical: levels of abstraction and complexity

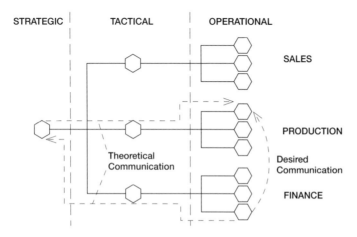

Figure 5-2   Hierarchical Organization

- Functional: different types of processes and functions

- Geographic: grouped by physical location

An enterprise is organized along several dimensions.

The vertical dimension reflects different levels of complexity of functions and processes. Jaques suggests that managerial hierarchies are the most natural and efficient form for large organizations and, properly structured, can release energy and creativity and improve morale [Jaques 1989]. He proposes that employees exercise judgment and discretion in performing processes having specified output quantity and quality within constraints of time and resources. At higher levels, the complexity of problem solving increases, and the level of work and the weight of responsibility reflect that complexity. To be successful, a person must have the right mental processes, a commitment to the type of work, and the skilled knowledge appropriate to the level of work.

Function and geography affect an organization.

A functional organization is divided into functional areas, whereas a process-centered organization is partitioned along the lines of its core business processes. The geographical dimension is strongly influenced by the quality of communication links between units. Poor communication requires that units have geographical autonomy, which might be better organized by process to minimize the splitting of responsibility and hand-offs between people, if communication is fast and reliable. Geography also has an impact for language, cultural, and social reasons. To gain advantage from these forms of organization, a corporation might have a manufacturing plant for each type of product, a sales office for each country in which it operates, and a procurement unit close to major suppliers.

Plan according to time horizons.

Organizations have business cycles at various levels (see Learning Organization on page 5). For example, forecasts and schedules differ according to time horizon: long-term forecasting of sales is typically done by product group and market segment; short-term scheduling is often done for individual products to specific customers. Figure 5-3 illustrates how processes affect entities according to

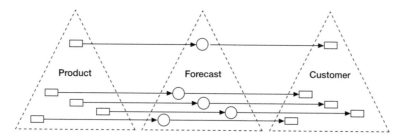

Figure 5-3   Hierarchical Process

their level of abstraction. Traditional command and control organizations progressively explode high-level plans into lower-level schedules for execution, and exercise control by aggregating and reporting results.

Network Organization

This hierarchical approach is flawed in that it does not reflect the exceedingly complex ways in which organizations interact in practice. Large conglomerates seek to manage hundreds or thousands of units, often distributed around the world. Large and small organizations work together to deliver value through complex networks of supply and demand. Activities that are not central to the business are outsourced to specialist entities, projects are formed and dispersed to achieve specific goals, and continuous change is the order of the day. The traditional "top-down" approach to managing through an organization hierarchy is neither feasible nor appropriate in such circumstances.

Modern business is exceedingly complex.

This type of complex system is recognized to have unpredictable, nonlinear, chaotic behavior, where even minute causes can have massive effects. Clausewitz noted that in war: "success is not due simply to general causes. Particular factors can often be decisive— details only known to those who were on the spot—while issues can be decided by chances and incidents so minute as to figure in histories simply as anecdotes" [Clausewitz 1984].

Complex systems are unpredictable and chaotic.

Discrete event simu-lation using agents has promise.

This phenomenom has also been widely observed in nature, and is the subject of the study of chaos, swarm behavior, and complex adaptive systems. Research aimed at unraveling the complexity of business systems continues, and is far from complete, but has promise as it embraces the self-management that characterizes learning organizations. Discrete event simulation tools such as Swarm illustrate the potential, but they are not yet widely available in a form that business people can use [Minar et al. 1996]. However, some promising work has been done in the fields of supply chain management [Teigen 1997] and concurrent engineering [Balasubramanian and Norrie 1996].

Complexity theory is a way of thinking about organizations.

Complexity theory is a way of thinking about the collective behavior of interacting units "from the bottom up." Instead of an organization being viewed as a large entity decomposed into smaller chunks, it is viewed as a collection of many collaborating units. Hierarchy is replaced by network to model the ways in which these relatively simple entities interact to achieve their ends. This swarm behavior is widely observed in nature but has only recently been recognized in business systems: "as we wire ourselves into a hivish network, many things will emerge that we, as mere neurons in the network, don't expect, don't understand, can't control, or don't even perceive" [Kelly 1994].

Organizations develop from units to groups to federations.

Figure 5-4 illustrates development of an organization from a single unit having internal management, through a group of units where interaction is external to the units but internal to the group, to a federation of units having no overall management. The significance of this progression is that there is no single point of authority and control in the federation. Instead of exercising authority by command and control, units communicate and coordinate their activities in order to achieve their ends.

Organization units collaborate to achieve goals.

This reality is expressed in the definition of a supply chain as "a network of autonomous or semi-autonomous business entities collectively responsible for procurement, manufacturing, and distribution

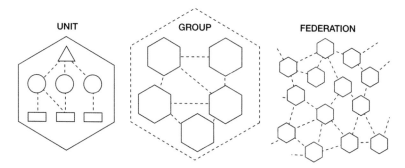

Figure 5-4   Organization Complexity

activities associated with one or more families of related products"
[Jayashankar et al. 1996]. Not only do supply chains typically exist
between organizations, but they are often transient. A virtual
enterprise is a temporary consortium or alliance of companies
formed to achieve a specific purpose. It shares costs, skills, and global market access to provide timely and competitive products and
services, which could not be achieved by any one of its individual

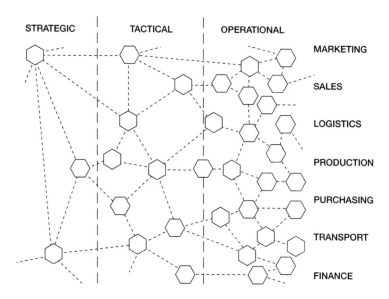

Figure 5-5   Network Organization

members [OMG 1997]. Large and complex business systems are therefore best implemented by networks of collaborating units, rather than by a centralized command authority (see Figure 5-6).

Centralized organizations have failure points.

Now emerging are new forms of organization for managing the complexity and scale of the modern business environment that are "purposely architected to distribute power, authority and control to the peripheral components" of their structure [Breuner 1995]. New processes evolve in response to change, some of which succeed, while others fail. Decentralized organizations survive such failures because they are diverse, but centralized systems are vulnerable to single points of failure that can prove fatal. A swarm of bees or colony of ants, for example, is not vulnerable to the death of a single insect. Diversity also enables organizations to exploit niches in which to survive and grow, in much the same way as plants adapt to specialized environments.

Autonomous Organizations

"Confronted with a task, and having less information available than is needed to perform that task, an organization may react in either of two ways. One is to increase its information processing capacity, the other to design the organization, and indeed the task itself, in such a way as to enable it to operate on the basis of less information. These approaches are exhaustive; no others are conceivable. A failure to adopt one or the other will automatically result in a drop in the level of performance" [Creveld 1985].

Modern thinking promotes decoupling of organizations.

Modern thinking is that communication and coordination between units should be minimized by maximizing their ability to manage themselves. Mintzberg [Mintzberg 1979] suggests that "the glue holding organizational structure together" progressively involves:

- Coordination of work by informal communication

- Coordination by someone responsible for the work of others

- Standardization of work processes

- Standardization of skills and knowledge

- Rules of behavior and shared values

- Standardization of outputs or results

The units of an organization that develop this glue have a high degree of autonomy. For example, standards of work and output remove the need for communication and control of each instance. Standardization of knowledge and rules of behavior lead to expectations of similar performance between units, reducing the need for their individual management.

Standards and knowledge promote autonomy.

"An organization is a network of interacting *agents* that create, maintain and terminate commitments" [Verharen 1997]. Complexity theory indicates that organizations can be modeled as collections of *intelligent agents* that collaborate and compete in order to achieve their goals. Intelligent agent technology has been applied with success in scientific, engineering, and business domains to model complex systems. As an organization unit manages its processes and entities to achieve its purpose, an intelligent agent manages its actions and knowledge to achieve its goals. As organization units collaborate to achieve shared purpose, agents communicate and coordinate their work to achieve mutual goals. Figure 5-6 illustrates how an organization unit receives requests for work from other units, and manages its internal processes and entities to satisfy the requests according to its purpose. The unit may in turn request services of other units to assist with its work—in much the same way as an intelligent agent operates.

Organizations may be modeled by intelligent agents.

This fact allows certain kinds of work to be automated. Automated processes are no different from other business processes except that they do not require human interaction. Many process steps can be automated by replacing human actions with a "script" of equivalent

Automated processes do not require human interaction.

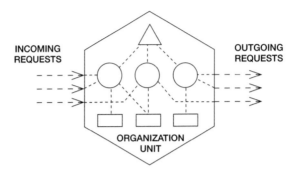

INCOMING
REQUESTS

OUTGOING
REQUESTS

ORGANIZATION
UNIT

Figure 5-6 Organization as Agent

computer actions. For example, an electronic purchase request does not need a human operator to enter vendor, product, and other order details. Furthermore, an order can be priced without human intervention by a pricing algorithm or table, and can then be forwarded to the next step according to process workflow rules.

A business process can be improved without major reengineering.

A business process can be improved without major reengineering by identifying those steps that can be automated and by automating them on a piecemeal basis. Indeed, this is exactly the incremental approach that has been adopted so successfully by Japanese manufacturers to achieve global leadership in many industries. Because it eliminates the need for large-scale process analysis, design and implementation, and associated change management, this approach has significantly less risk than traditional reengineering exercises. Many small improvements can be gained without significant investment or risk, and can be phased according to available resources.

Automatic processes are carried out by automated roles.

Process automation is enabled within a workflow framework by creating an *automated role* that is responsible for automating process steps. Since any process may be automated, all process steps are initially allocated to the automated role. If the step is automated, it is executed by the automated role; otherwise, it is transferred to the workpool of an equivalent human role. If the process step can be done without human intervention, it executes and transfers control to the

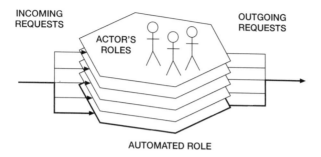

INCOMING
REQUESTS

OUTGOING
REQUESTS

ACTOR'S
ROLES

AUTOMATED ROLE

Figure 5-7   Organization Unit and Roles

next step. Each process step is supervised by a human role to which control is passed only if the process cannot execute automatically.

A human actor then intervenes in the process to take appropriate action. If the intervention is routine and can be reduced to a rule, then the automatic aspect of the process is extended or refined to handle future instances without human intervention. In this way, an organization effectively gains knowledge and progressively reduces the *workload* of its human users while simultaneously improving the quality and consistency of their work. This kind of process automation uses many of the concepts of intelligent agents, and uses them in a complementary fashion. Indeed, an organization unit may be thought of as a set of agents performing both human and automated roles (see Figure 5-7).

Automated processes are supervised by humans.

Coordination of Organizations

Autonomous organizations coordinate their activities through shared purpose, either by a power relationship in which one can exercise authority over others or by contracts (see Purpose and Contract on page 49). A contract is the result of a negotiation process; thereafter, requests are made and fulfilled according to the terms of the contract by communications between the parties to the contract. This requires that the organization be able to manage contracts and communicate with other parties.

A contract is the result of a negotiation process.

Contracts enable autonomous units to cooperate.

Contracts enable units to cooperate while retaining substantial autonomy. This does not entirely remove the need for coordination, because obligations in terms of the contracts must still be incurred and fulfilled. This is done by messages that initiate local processes and notify their completion according to contract clauses. A greater dependency occurs if workflow is both within and between units, because this implies that all units are participating in a single process, which is typically under the control of a supervisory unit.

One unit imposes obligations on another.

An organization unit may be completely autonomous, managing its processes and resources to achieve its goals independently of any other influence. More frequently, however, a unit has to coordinate its work with the work of others to achieve shared purpose. To do this, a customer unit must be able to impose obligations on a supplier unit, either by having power over the supplier or by enforcing the terms of a contract between them. Power relationships are typical of organizations that use command and control to achieve purpose, such as the military. Contracts, conventions, codes of practice, and relevant laws are the means by which truly autonomous units collaborate.

A contract defines policies for situations.

A contract is modeled by a specialized state transition diagram called a contract diagram (see Contract Components on page 159). The actions to be taken in every possible state of affairs are defined in contract clauses, including the contract's fulfillment, cancellation, and violation. Each results in another state of affairs coming into effect, ultimately the termination of the contract. The clauses oblige, permit, or forbid each party to perform processes in terms of the contract, where permission and prohibition are types of authorization. The appropriate process may be instantiated in terms of the contract and, when completed, results in a new state of affairs.

Organization and Communication

Organizations communicate by speech acts.

Organizations communicate through messages based on *speech act* theory in much the same way as humans communicate, which requires that they share a language, an *ontology,* and a protocol. The language is the syntax of the communication, and the ontology is the vocabulary or lexicon that defines the meanings of words. The protocol is the convention used to establish, maintain, and terminate the communication. A contract defines the speech acts to which a party can respond, and a contract manager enforces the contract. There are analogies between this model and Meyer's concepts of software contracts [Meyer 1988], but enterprise contracts, messages, and transactions typically have <u>legal</u> as well as operational implications.

Simple point-to-point communication is suitable if the address of each party is known, and broadcasting to a specific community is suitable if it is of reasonable size. Interested parties can also subscribe to services that provide specific kinds of messages. Otherwise, communication facilitators may be used to broker, recruit, or recommend business partners. Procurement brokers and "yellow pages" help find suppliers of goods and services; bulletin boards advise of requests for quotation; and specialized markets facilitate trade among individuals and companies.

Facilitators broker, recruit, and recommend products and services.

For example, a purchase process might send a request for quotation to an individual supplier, to a list of selected suppliers, to all suppliers within a certain distance, or to all suppliers that have registered an ability to supply the desired item. Naturally, such messages must be understood by other units, whether or not they use the same systems, or even speak the same language. This is a critical requirement of value chains that operate as much between as within organizations, and where systems are composed of applications from different vendors. It requires that they have the ability to exchange information at the <u>business</u> level as well as at the technological level.

Messages must be understood by different systems.

Many organizations have business systems that should be able to interoperate automatically through suitable business and technological standards, but this is not yet widely feasible. First, there are

Business standards are needed.

as yet no globally accepted business ontologies or vocabularies; second, object interaction based on static interfaces is vulnerable to business complexity and change; third, much of the world does not yet have secure and reliable networks to support such systems. Systems that use flexible and adaptable business-to-business communication to replace or extend existing *electronic data interchange* standards are likely to emerge. In particular, those that are able to structure the performative and semantic data required to coordinate disparate organizations will succeed.

Value Networks

Messages communicate information and requests for services.

As described above, messages communicate information and requests for services between organizations. Instead of relying on a central controller to manage subsidiaries, autonomous units coordinate their activities by agreeing how to achieve mutual goals. Negotiation establishes contracts, conventions, and hierarchies of authority that govern trading relationships between units, which enable units to elicit obligations, or commitments, from each other. A purchasing contract, for example, enables a customer to oblige a supplier to deliver products or services at a specified price and lead time.

One unit imposes an obligation on another.

When required, the unit directs the supplier, by means of a purchase order, to deliver such a product or service. The supplier accepts the obligation and adds it to its schedule, or agenda, of work to be done, in priority sequence. The obligation is fulfilled by performing the relevant business process, or is violated, in which case other obligations are typically incurred. Obligations are thus a form of dynamic purpose, continuously changing as they are imposed, fulfilled, and violated. The process schedules, allocates, and uses resources, and, if necessary, imposes obligations on other units. This continues along the supply chain for all required products and services.

Problems occur if there is insufficient capacity.

Problems occur with this approach, and with any other, when there is insufficient capacity or lead time for proper fulfillment of the obligation. This is a situation in which demand exceeds supply, and is managed in exactly the same way as in an open market. The strategy that the unit adopts is to maximize the values of the obligations that it intends to fulfill, thereby choosing to violate those of lesser value. Note that this value is not necessarily only financial value, but can include other measures such as customer satisfaction and management preferences. This market model is observed in the success of free market economies over command economies, and in the dominance of modern forces over traditional armies [Sander 1997].

Intelligent agents have been used to evaluate this form of coordination. Teigen successfully developed a supply chain management system having agents for marketing, planning, purchasing, inventory, production, and dispatching, which interacts with customers, suppliers, and other agents. Note the close parallel between his choice of agents and the units found in a typical manufacturing organization [Teigen 1997]. Intelligent agents have also been used for concurrent engineering [Balasubramanian and Norrie 1996] and in agile manufacturing [Matthews 1996]. These systems are illustrated by the simple value chain shown in Figure 5-8. The sales office agent records and acknowledges orders received from customers and adds them to its order backlog. Each day (or other suitable interval), a message is sent to the agent representing the distribution unit to request the back-ordered products. If the unit has sufficient inventory, it records its delivery to the customer and notifies the sales office, which in turn creates and communicates a sales invoice.

Intelligent agents will become commonplace.

If there is not enough distribution inventory, the unit requests replenishment product from the production facility to satisfy back orders and safety stock in accordance with its stocking policies. The request is batched with others to be scheduled for production when there is sufficient material and capacity. A purchase request is sent to the procurement agent if material is to be purchased, which hopefully results in receipt of the goods by the production facility.

Agents respond to and issue requests.

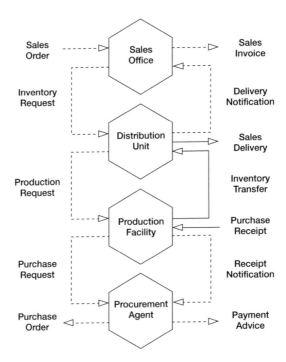

Figure 5-8 Organization and Messages

Each agent is then notified as production is completed and delivered through the distribution unit to the customer.

Each agent deals only with its immediate peers.

A unit in this model deals only with its immediate peers, with no centralized planning. A unit is expert in a particular domain and knows nothing of other domains except the protocol by which to exchange information. Naturally, should there be agents representing the customers, suppliers, and banks, they would also communicate by appropriate messages. The purpose of each unit in this type of system is to manage its own processes and resources as well as it can in order to respond to requests from other units. This is unlikely to be globally optimal, but it should be sufficiently effective to justify the substantially reduced complexity of such decentralized, autonomous units.

Organization Components

Organization components are the elements of an enterprise that are responsible for managing purpose, process, and entity components. Management within an organization is typically carried out by planning and control of the work of actors, and management between organizations is done by communication and coordination of work in terms of agreements. Organizations manage parties and actors, definitions and instances of the processes that they can perform, and their business entities. An organization component may itself be an entity in an enterprise model at a higher level of abstraction.

*Organization compo-
nents manage other
components.*

Organization Unit

The organization unit is the primary component of an organization, providing a context for its management. Organization structure relates a parent unit to its subsidiaries in a hierarchy, and each unit is responsible for collections of other business components. A unit that has legal status is a party, because it is able to contract with other parties to achieve its purpose. Interaction between units is governed by contracts, which are administered by a contract manager. Work is done by means of processes that are instantiated

*An organization unit
provides a manage-
ment context.*

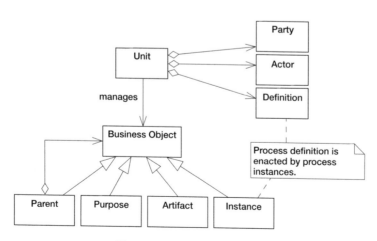

Figure 5-9 Organization Unit

either by actors or by requests made by other parties in terms of these contracts. Workflow between actors is managed within a unit by a process manager, and between units by a message manager. The process manager routes work to actors according to their organization roles, while the message manager communicates requests and responses to other parties. Finally, an entity manager locates and allocates the entities affected by the business processes.

Organization Role

Process instances are assigned to actors. An organization role is the means by which business process instances are assigned to actors, and vice versa. A "push" system allocates a process step to an actor when it is started, while a "pull" system allocates it to an actor with the appropriate role when the actor requests work (see Actor on page 106). In a pull system, the actor must know which roles it can perform, while a push system requires an organization role to know its actors. A pull system is typically implemented by a workpool of work items (instances of process steps) for each role, from which actors request work. A push system is implemented by a worklist for each actor, into which work items are scheduled.

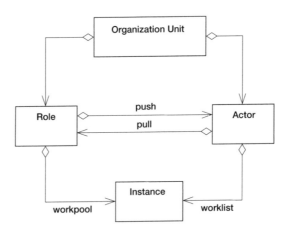

Figure 5-10   Actors and Roles

Contract Components

Contracts define the behavior agreed and expected between parties having a shared purpose (see Purpose and Contract on page 49). A contract is instantiated as a set of obligations between its parties, which are either fulfilled, canceled, or violated. A contract defines the rights and obligations in every possible case, including violation, which is illustrated in Figure 5-11 for a hypothetical vehicle reservation contract [Breu et al. 1997].

A contract defines expected behavior.

Just as a contract has a clause that specifies the course of action in any situation, a contract diagram represents it through its *deontic* states and the conditions that relate them. This is a specialization of a state transition diagram, where each state and its transitions represent a clause in the contract. It is important to realize that the contract does not describe the vehicle reservation process, but rather the rights and obligations of each party, which govern the process. Not only does this have legal implications, but it also enables an otherwise complex process to be clearly partitioned between the parties. Figure 5-12 highlights quite unambiguously the burden of obligation carried by the booking office in this contract [Verharen 1997].

Contracts are modeled by means of deontic states and speech acts.

Vehicle Reservation Contract

Parties to the agreement are:
ABC Travel, hereinafter the Travel Agent;
DEF Hire, hereinafter the Booking Office; and
GHI Motors, hereinafter the Vehicle Depot.

1) The Travel Agent may request vehicles to be reserved by the Booking Office.
2) The Booking Office shall check with the Vehicle Depot to determine if the requested vehicle is available.
3) The Vehicle Depot shall advise the Booking Office that the vehicle either is, or is not, available.
4) Should the vehicle not be available, the reservation request shall be rejected.
5) If the vehicle is available, the Booking Office shall offer it to the Travel Agent at the current retail price.
6) The Travel Agent shall either accept or reject the offer.
7) Should the offer be accepted, the Booking Office shall confirm the reservation with the Vehicle Depot.
8) Finally, should the offer be rejected, the reservation is to be cancelled.

Signed at _____ on _____ by _____ _____ _____

Figure 5-11 Vehicle Reservation Contract

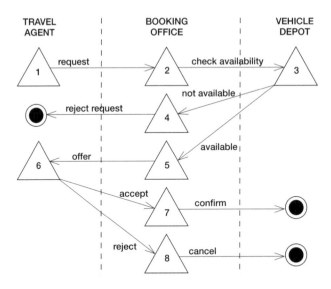

Figure 5-12   Contract Diagram

Contracts enable speech acts to be identified.

Analysis of the contract also enables the nature of the speech acts between the parties to be clearly identified. The initial request by the travel agent, for example, is a directive, while the response of the vehicle depot is a declaration. Its deontic states represent how things ought to be, and so are direct expressions of purpose and are, at the lowest level, measurable entity values. A business process is designed to provide transition between these states, and so is the means by which an organization fulfills its purpose.

A customer may impose an obligation on a supplier.

A customer who is authorized in terms of the contract may impose an obligation on a supplier by sending the appropriate message. The contract itself can also create an obligation in the absence of a message if a predefined state is reached. For example, a maintenance process might be invoked after a particular interval has elapsed or when a specific condition obtains. Unfulfilled obligations are listed in the unit's master schedule, typically in priority sequence. A process for fulfilling an obligation is released, when due and if feasible, by the process manager. Should the process be unfeasible, or fail for some reason, the contract manager handles the violation according to the rules laid down in the contract. This may be done by instantiating a corrective process or by advising the customer of the violation, or both.

The ability of XML to structure a document, and to tag its content with semantic labels, provides the opportunity to integrate policies and the processes by which they are enforced. To illustrate this, the vehicle reservation contract shown in Figure 5-11 has been translated into an equivalent XML document in Figure 5-13. The textual

Documents may be tagged with semantic labels.

```
<CONTRACT> VehicleReservationContract
  <PARTY> entity.role.party.TravelAgent
    <PERMIT> 1
      <DESCRIPTION>The Travel Agent may request vehicles...</DESCRIPTION>
      <FULFILL>2</FULFILL>
    </PERMIT>
    <OBLIGE> 6
      <DESCRIPTION>The Travel Agent shall either accept ...</DESCRIPTION>
      <FULFILL>7</FULFILL>
      <VIOLATE>8</VIOLATE>
    </OBLIGE>
  </PARTY>
  <PARTY> entity.role.party.BookingOffice
    <OBLIGE> 2
      <DESCRIPTION>The Booking Office shall check with ...</DESCRIPTION>
      <FULFILL>3</FULFILL>
    </OBLIGE>
    <OBLIGE> 4
      <DESCRIPTION>Should the vehicle not be available, ...</DESCRIPTION>
      <FULFILL>END</FULFILL>
    </OBLIGE>
    ....
  </PARTY>
  <PARTY> entity.role.party.VehicleDept
    <OBLIGE> 3
      <DESCRIPTION>The Vehicle Depot shall advise the...</DESCRIPTION>
      <FULFILL>5</FULFILL>
      <VIOLATE>4</VIOLATE>
    </OBLIGE>
  </PARTY>
</CONTRACT>
```

Figure 5-13 XML Contract

form of the document can be reconstructed from the description sections, including its party and clause elements. Each contract has a name and two or more party sections, each of which is also named, and contains one or more clauses. The types of clauses include permission, prohibition, and obligation, each defining a right or obligation of a party. The actions that flow from a state of affairs include fulfill, violate, and cancel, each of which causes another state of affairs by instantiating a process. Because the contract is shared between two or more units, it is implemented independently of any particular organization. An XML document is an effective means by which to communicate the contract among the parties, including entities that aspire to any of the roles, without binding it to any particular party. Each unit extracts only those conditions that appertain to it, for use by its contract manager.

Contract Manager

Customers make requests in terms of a contract.

The contract manager has two fundamental responsibilities—first as customer, and second as performer—in the fulfillment of the purpose of the contract. The customer role recommends suitable parties given a purpose—for example, suppliers that are able to deliver a particular product or service—typically in response to requests from the process manager. Should there be a suitable party, the request is communicated to the party by the message manager. Should there be more than one party potentially able to satisfy the request, several may be asked to respond.

A performer must respond in terms of the contract.

The customer is authorized to make the request, and the performer is obliged to respond, in terms of a contract between them. The request might include details of the specific products, quantities, delivery dates, and other relevant information. The performer may in turn request performance from other parties to help satisfy the request, thereby developing a supply chain. This typically requires that the parties in the chain negotiate the condition and timing of supply to meet demand. Note that each unit is interested only in its immediate customers and suppliers, and that no one manages the whole supply chain.

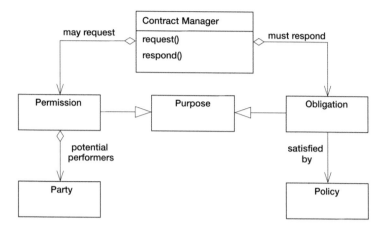

Figure 5-14   Contract Manager

Figure 5-15 illustrates the (much simplified) actions required to communicate a request by the process manager to suitable parties, and to manage their responses. The actions by the other party, or performer, are similarly illustrated in Figure 5-16. The performer

The performer applies a policy in terms of the contract.

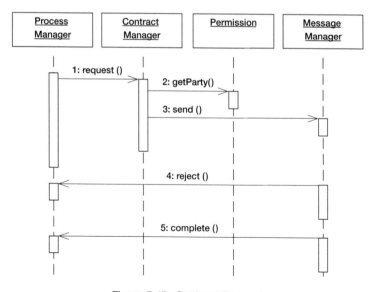

Figure 5-15   Contract Request

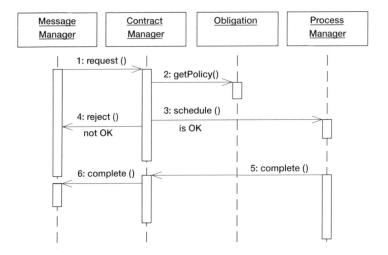

Figure 5-16   Contract Response

receives the request and decides the policy it is to apply in terms of
the contract. This may be to reject the request (for example, if it has
insufficient capacity or lead time), or to request its process manager
to instantiate and schedule a process to satisfy the request. On completion of the process, the performer's message manager communicates the fact to the customer's message manager, which in turn
advises its process manager. This completes the workflow loop from
request to satisfaction—but between autonomous parties, not
merely between roles within one organization (see Workflow Loop
on page 59).

Supply is pegged to
demand so that
changes can be
propagated.

Supply is pegged to demand by way of the obligations that link the
units, so changes can be propagated in both directions along the
supply chain. For example, the impact of a quality defect in a batch
of component parts can immediately be fed forward to reschedule
the affected downstream products. Similarly, the effect of a canceled,
reconfigured, or reprioritized order is immediately propagated to its
upstream suppliers. The effect of changing priorities is minimized
because each party need replan only if it cannot meet dates specified by the new schedule.

Process Manager

A process manager responds to requests for work by creating an instance of the appropriate process and adding it to the workpool of the appropriate organization role. A process step that requires human interaction is allocated to the appropriate role to be done by a person who is assigned that role. When complete, the process step is transferred to a list of completed processes, which is an audit trail of work completed. The process manager also records the average cycle time—the duration from creation to completion—of each process type.

Processes are instantiated and scheduled.

Workflow depends on organization roles to group work items to be performed by each type of actor. An organization unit therefore has a collection of roles, each having a list of work items that must be done. The process manager responds to a request for work by obtaining the appropriate process definition and role, creating a new instance of the process, and adding it to the worklist of the role. The sequence of these actions is illustrated in Figure 5-18.

Process workflow depends on roles.

Processes can be automated by adding to each organization role an "automatic" workpool containing processes that can be executed without human intervention. These processes are allocated to the automatic workpool to be executed immediately (or at a prespecified time, or after a specified delay). For example, a purchase process typically requires approval, usually by different roles according to the

Certain process steps can be automated.

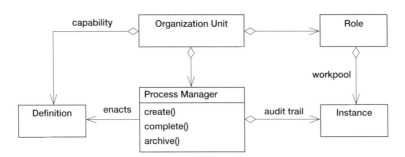

Figure 5-17 Process Manager

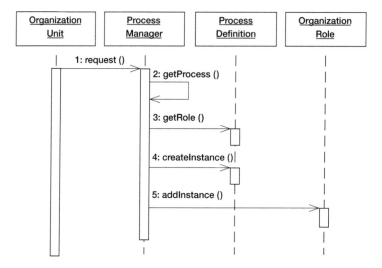

Figure 5-18   Instantiate Process

purchase value and purpose. Often the cost of approval exceeds the purchase value, and so should be automated to approve the request if below a predefined value. When such a process is instantiated, its

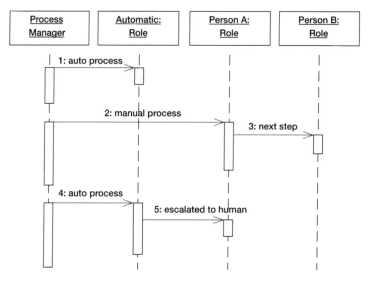

Figure 5-19   Process Automation

role determines if it can be executed automatically, or whether it requires human intervention, and the process manager starts and executes the step. Should this fail for any reason, the process is transferred to the manual worklist to be performed by its human actor, which in effect is its supervisor (see Figure 5-19).

Message Manager

An organization unit exchanges messages with its peers and other parties such as customers, suppliers, and financial and regulatory institutions. Such messages are based on speech act theory, using standard vocabularies to enable interaction with other businesses. A message header typically identifies the speech act by a verb/noun combination such as "POST JOURNAL," the message version number, a transport and destination address, whether and by when an acknowledgment is required, and the vocabulary (or lexicon or ontology) used to encode the message contents. The contents of a message are typically in XML [OA9 1997].

An organization communicates with other parties.

The manager tracks outgoing messages waiting to be sent to and acknowledged by the recipient; messages that have not yet been acknowledged; mapping of noun, verb, and version attributes of

Messages implement speech acts.

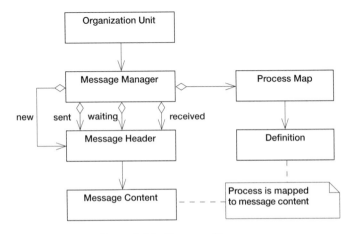

Figure 5-20   Message Manager

messages onto the equivalent process names; and outgoing messages that have not been sent. Business messages often have monetary and legal value, so it is necessary to know whether they have been received and, if they have been broadcast, by how many recipients. In most situations, however, it is not feasible for a process to wait for a reply before continuing with other work, and so acknowledgments must be managed explicitly.

An outgoing message is initiated by a process. Figure 5-21 illustrates the sequence of actions performed by the message manager in sending a message based on a business process instance. The recipient's address is obtained from the relevant party, and the verb/noun/version and format of the message are obtained from the process map. A new message header is created with this information, and its message contents encodes the process state with the appropriate format, language, and vocabulary. The message is added to the outgoing message queue, and a placeholder is created if the message is to be acknowledged by the recipient.

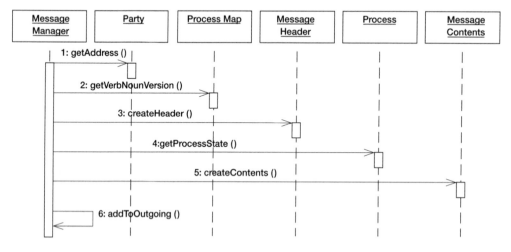

Figure 5-21   Send Message

The reverse obtains when a message is received by the message manager. The process associated with the message's noun, verb, and version is instantiated, initiated with the attribute values contained in the message contents, and added to the worklist of the appropriate organization role. Thereafter, it behaves in exactly the same way as a local process instance. Business processes are performed as much between as within organizations and flow through different business systems, typically being recreated manually in each system. Previous attempts to chain processes using EDI and EFT have not been widely adopted because they require that the senders and receivers of messages agree to an exact message format.

Processes are initiated by incoming messages.

Any change in a format must be agreed to by all participants, making such approaches inflexible and brittle. Sims argues that the problem can be avoided by "semantic data streams" that label each data element in a message, which allows a system to extract and interpret only those items in which it is interested [Sims 1994].

Semantic data streams enable loose coupling between systems.

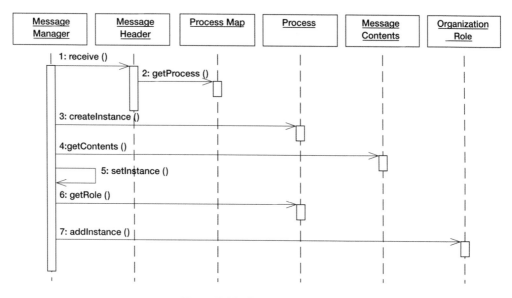

Figure 5-22 Receive Message

Knowing the name and type of the incoming data item, it can perform whatever transformations are needed to condition it for internal use. A system can similarly label its outgoing data for the benefit of others.

XML is a language for describing complex data.

XML has emerged as a powerful, nonproprietary language for describing complex data [W3C 1997], and so is an ideal means by which to implement semantic messages. For disparate systems to communicate the meanings of such messages, they must agree to use a common vocabulary, or ontology. Different domains require different ontologies, even within industry and commerce, and certainly among scientific, military, and governmental organizations. The components described in this section enable a process in one organization to start a process in another without the two processes having any direct knowledge of each other. Complex systems that would otherwise need to be tightly integrated, and therefore inflexible, can be replaced by simple systems loosely coupled by semantic messages.

Entity Manager

The organization allocates entities to its processes.

The entity manager uses various techniques to select and allocate suitable entities to each process (see Names and Identity of an Entity on page 100). A human actor who knows the identity or name of an entity can select it from a list or tree of suitable candidates. Alternatively, the entity manager can select or suggest entities according to their types and relevant attributes. Much of this behavior can be delegated to the entities themselves, which are organized typically in a hierarchy by name or type and are indexed by identity. Each entity role also maintains a list of values that it can access, enabling individual process steps to operate directly on them (see Actions on page 14).

Summary

Organizations have developed over many centuries to manage the increasingly complex economic, government, religious, and military worlds. Global business now demands radically distributed systems that operate as much between as within organizations. The value networks that connect suppliers and customers have no central point of control, and so require new forms of management.

Complexity theory provides some indication of how this is to be achieved. Central to the coordination of otherwise autonomous organizations is the contract, a concept that has survived many centuries of use in business and government. Business systems can be created that interpret and apply the rules defined in formal contracts. With such contracts in place, the command and control required of current enterprise software can be replaced by systems of coordination and communication.

This requires standards for contracts and messages at the business level, including ontologies or lexicons defining the meanings of words used in such documents. It also requires software that can interpret contracts and messages and take appropriate actions to synchronize the business processes of the units involved. Should this occur, it will precipitate a profound revolution in the way business is done and will dramatically change the nature of enterprise systems.

Appendix

Simple System

The simple system illustrates some of the concepts described in this book, and is partially implemented by the Java code listed in the CD-ROM. The class diagram below shows how the main entity (role) and process classes are related to form a value chain linking sales, production, purchasing, payment and payroll, and finance activities. This is a small subset of a real enterprise system, but may satisfy the needs of a small business.

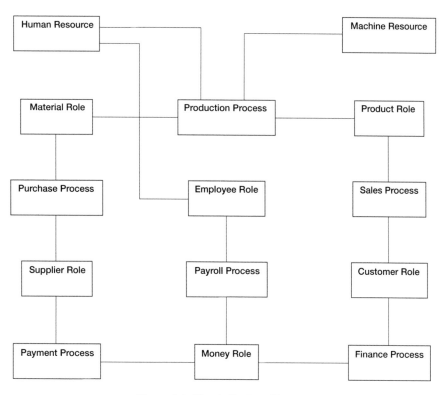

Figure A-1 Simple System Diagram

Entity Components

Customer Role

A customer is described by its company details (or personal details if it is an individual), contacted by means of its postal and electronic addresses, and accounted for by its receivable account. The receivable account is its most important property in this model—debited during the sales process and credited in the finance process. The generic role has a unique identity and the hierarchical structure by which a customer is located (see Names and Identity of an Entity on page 100).

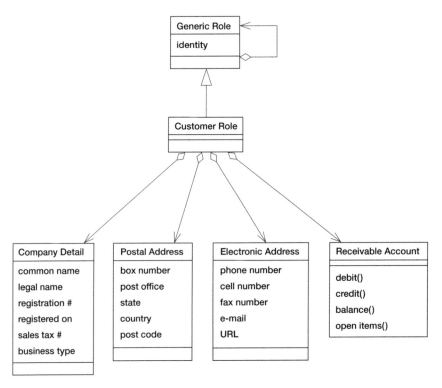

Figure A-2   Customer Role

Employee Role

An employee is described by its personal details, contacted by its postal address, and paid through its EFT address according to the amounts accrued in its payroll account. The employee role is not concerned with abilities or useful capacity, which are the concerns of the person's human resource role.

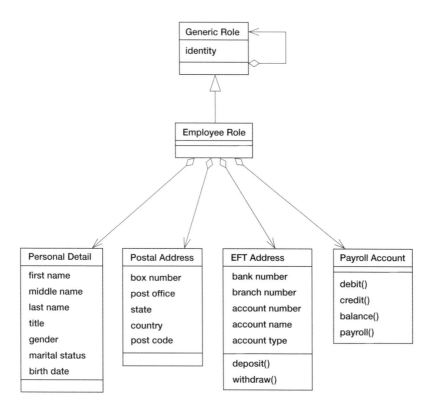

Figure A-3   Employee Role

Human Resource

A human resource has personal details (equivalent to those of an employee), a list of abilities describing what kind of work the person can do, and the person's capacity to do such work. A human resource is typically able to do only one job at a time, and so its capacity is modeled by the monopolized value (see Capacity on page 121).

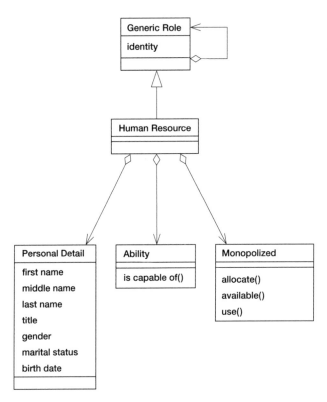

Figure A-4 Human Resource

Machine Resource

A machine resource is similarly modeled by its description, abilities, and capacity. Since a machine is able to work only on one piece at a time, its capacity is also of the monopolized type. This enables both human and machine resources to behave in the same way with respect to processes requiring capacity (see Production Process on page 188).

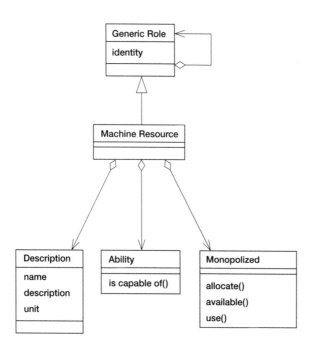

Figure A-5   Machine Resource

Material Role

Material is the name given to the raw materials, parts, components, and consumable items that are used in a production process, which in turn may be products of other processes. Material has specification, price, inventory, and cost accounts in this model. Different specifications of the same material may be required for technical, shipping, storage, and safety purposes. Price may vary among currencies, suppliers, and locations (see Price on page 130). Inventory is an optional property for material that is stocked, which is accounted for by the cost account.

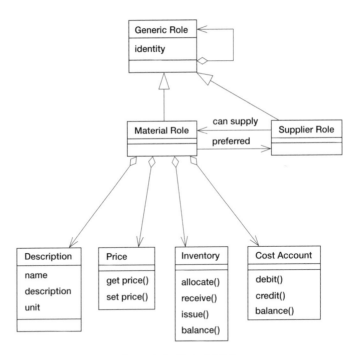

Figure A-6   Material Role

Money Role

Money is typically held in a current or investment account at a financial institution, and is modeled by the company details of the institution, its electronic address, and the EFT address of the account at the institution. A control account is needed to track all monetary transactions so that they can be reconciled and audited. Note that the account at the institution is distinctly different from the internal bank account.

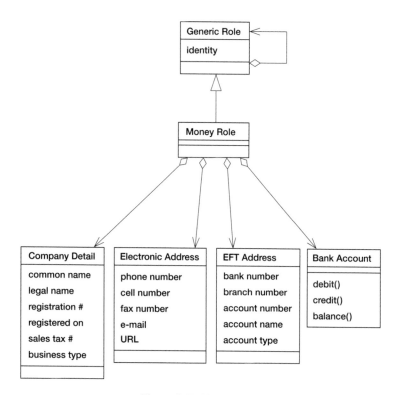

Figure A-7   Money Role

Product Role

A product is similar to material, except that it also has a product structure (or bill of materials) to define its components and to calculate its cost(s) from those of its components. A product may also define the production process by which it is made, although this may be the responsibility of other components (see Contract Manager on page 162).

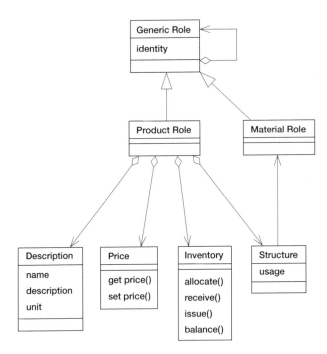

Figure A-8 Product Role

Supplier Role

A supplier is described by its company (or personal) details, contacted by its postal and electronic addresses, and accounted for by
its payable account. This model of a supplier is almost identical to
that of a customer, and they might be merged into a single component in many situations. Of course, a single entity may be both a
customer and a supplier.

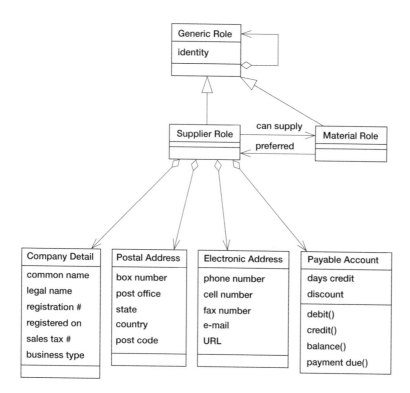

Figure A-9   Supplier Role

Process Components

Finance Process

A process interacts with entity roles, and process steps change entity values (see Actions on page 14). In this example, the statement lists balances and open items from a customer's receivable account. The dunning step draws similar information for formatting into a suitable dunning letter or message.

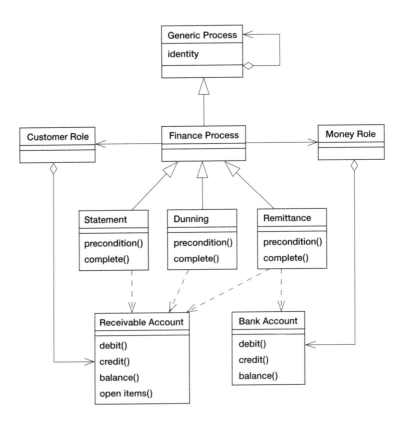

Figure A-10   Finance Process

The remittance step records payment by the customer both in the receivable account and in the bank account to which it is (to be) deposited. The precondition checks that the customer has a receivable account, raising an exception if not. The complete operation then gets balances and open items from the account, formats them with the customer's address, and sends the statement.

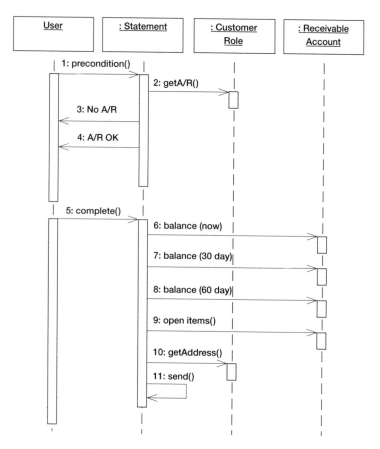

Figure A-11 Statement Sequence Division

Payment Process

The payment process has a single step that determines from the payable account the amount due for payment (according to the credit terms and discount allowed) and makes payment from the specified bank account. The `payment()` method calculates the amount due for payment, the `precondition()` method checks whether or not the process can be completed, and the `complete()` method credits the payable account, debits the bank account, and pays the amount due according to the `payment type`.

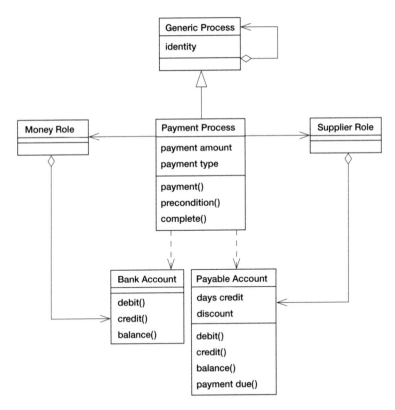

Figure A-12 Payment Process

The `payment()` method gets the supplier's account payable property to determine the balance to be paid according to its payment
terms and to set the payment amount to the amount due. The
`precondition()` method gets the payable and bank accounts to
which the amount is to be posted, and the `complete()` method
debits the account payable, and credits the bank account, with the
payment amount. Finally, the paid items are matched to the payment process, which is in effect their batch process, and are then
removed from the list of open items of the account (see Account on
page 113).

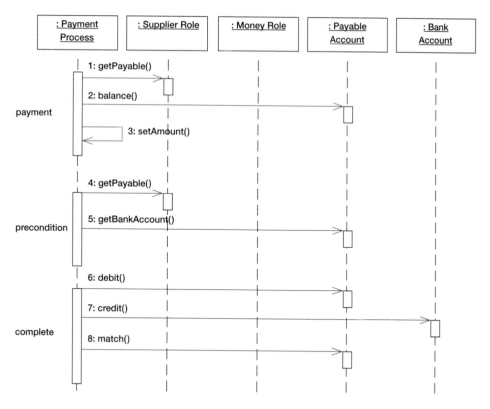

Figure A-13 Payment Sequence Diagram

Payroll Process

The accrual step of the payroll process determines the amount to be paid to an employee, including earnings, benefits, deductions, and other pay items in its payroll account, and the tax payable is calculated by an income tax account. Its `complete()` method credits both the payroll and tax accounts. The payroll account is debited and the bank account credited in the payroll settle step, when the employee is paid. The tax account is typically debited by a payment process when the tax is paid to the Internal Revenue Service, much like any other supplier. The two sequence diagrams illustrate the flow of events caused by each payroll process step, initially accruing the payroll and tax amounts and then paying (settling) the payroll.

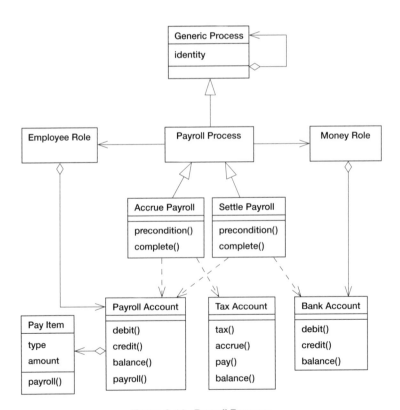

Figure A-14 Payroll Process

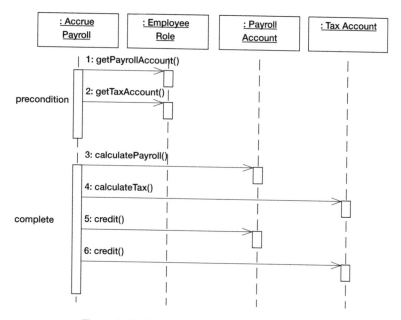

Figure A-15   Accrue Payroll Sequence Diagram

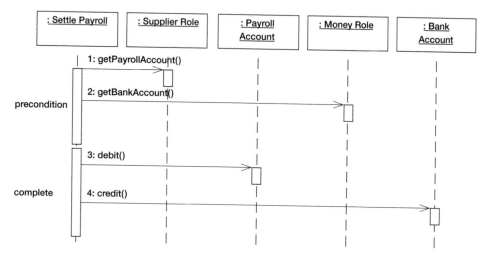

Figure A-16   Settle Payroll Sequence Diagram

Production Process

A production process typically has a longer duration than those of the sales, purchase, payroll, and other processes described in this section (see Work in Process on page 84). It is supported in this by

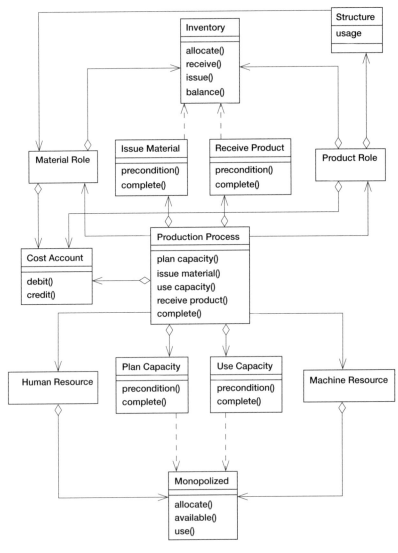

Figure A-17   Production Process

subprocesses for planning and recording the issue of material, the use of human and machine resources, and the receipt of product. Other subprocesses might track quality defects, lost time, material waste, tool usage, and relevant documentation. The production process identifies the product(s) to be made, and the materials required are defined by the product structures. On issue, the inventory and cost of material are reduced (or credited), and the process cost is debited by the equivalent amount. The production process has methods for enacting the subprocesses as required, and for completing the process as a whole.

The way in which material is issued is illustrated in the first sequence diagram below, where the quantities of materials required are calculated from the product structure and production quantity and are compared with the inventory balance of each (at the appropriate location). If available, the material is issued to the process as illustrated in the second sequence diagram, updating inventory and WIP cost accounts.

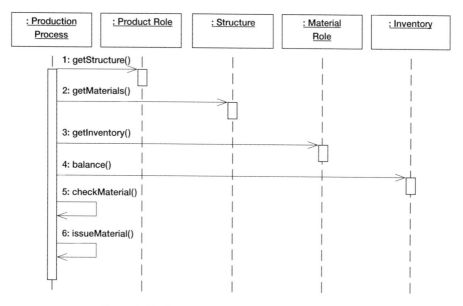

Figure A-18 Production Process Sequence Diagram

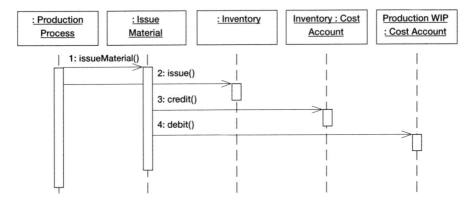

Figure A-19   Production Issue Sequence Diagram

Capacity planning allocates a human and/or machine resource for (part of) the duration of the process and deallocates the capacity when used. Receipt of product credits the process cost account with its value, debiting its cost account in turn. The product cost account is an inventory account for a make-to-stock process and a cost of sales account for a make-to-order process. When the production process is completed, the residual balance of the process cost account, which is a WIP account on the balance sheet, is typically transferred to a production cost variance account in the income statement.

Purchase Process

The purchase process is used to acquire products, which may be goods or services, from suppliers. The request step identifies or describes the product to be purchased and invites one or more preferred suppliers to quote. The quote step creates or updates the price of the product, either selecting the best price or recording that of each supplier (and perhaps other criteria such as order quantity). The order step confirms an order with a supplier and allocates the planned quantity to an inventory if it is to be stocked. Finally, the receipt step deallocates and receives the product into inventory if stocked, and debits the material cost account and credits the supplier's payable account with the purchase value. The cost account is

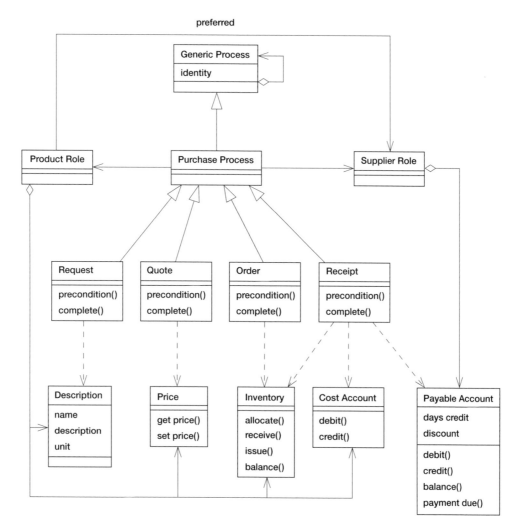

Figure A-20   Pruchase Process

typically an expense or consumable account if the material is not to be stocked.

The purchase receipt process `precondition()` method acquires the appropriate inventory and the inventory cost and supplier's payable accounts. The `complete()` method updates the inventory

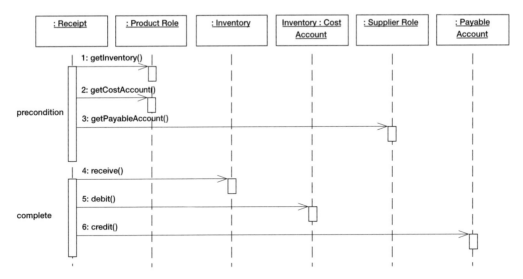

Figure A-21   Purchase Receipt Sequence Diagram

balance by means of its `receive()` method and debits its cost
account with the value of inventory received. The supplier's payable account is credited with the equivalent value in this example.
A more sophisticated model might allow for cost variances, input
tax accrual, receipt into quarantine inventory pending inspection,
and so on. Inventory might be refined to cater for serial batch or
item numbering, integral lots, shelf life, evaporation, and other specialized needs. This process interaction model, however, remains
substantially unchanged.

Sales Process

The sales process is similar to the purchase process, having steps for
quote order and delivery. On delivery, inventory is issued (if an
inventory sale) and the cost (of inventory, WIP, or service) is credited, and the customer's receivable account is debited by the sale
value. Other options are required for cash sales, to record gross
profit, sales taxes, and so on. These options are typically implemented using accounts of various types to record the exchange of
value in the sale.

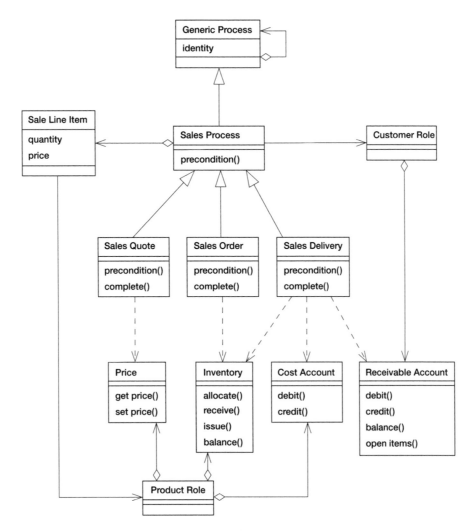

Figure A-22   Sales Process

Purpose Components

Production Schedule

This example is a much simplified form of a master production schedule and materials requirements planning (MPS/MRP) system, which excludes capacity planning. The schedule iterates through all manufactured products to determine if their inventory balances are below preset minimum levels, and, if so, creates objectives to replenish the inventories. Each MPS quantity is typically rounded up to a minimum order size and order multiple. The second (MRP) phase then calculates when the objective can be met, which in this model depends on when there are enough component materials to make the planned quantity of the product. The schedule uses the product's structure to determine the earliest time when sufficient inventory of all its components will be available using the `availableWhen()` method.

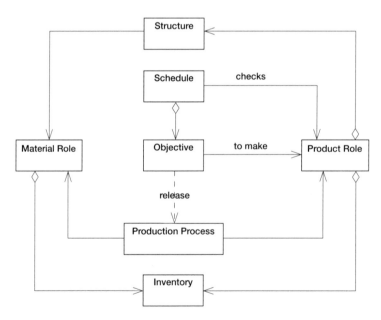

Figure A-23 Production Schedule

The sequence diagram below illustrates the flow of events in three distinct phases: first, to define the objectives (what is to be made, or MPS); second, to schedule the objectives and plan the resources (when it can be done, or MRP); and, finally, to release a production process to fulfill the objective, at which time the inventory of material that is required is allocated to the process. This ensures that it is no longer available to other processes and will be available for issue to the process when required. Naturally, the same principles can be applied to scheduling and allocation of other resources such as people, machines, tools, and specifications.

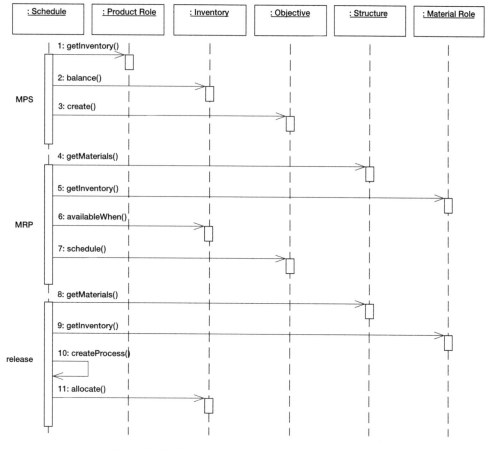

Figure A-24   Production Schedule Sequence Diagram

Financial Ledger

In this model, a general ledger is used to budget, measure, and summarize the financial value of the enterprise (see Financial Ledger on page 38). While this is mandatory for statutory income tax purposes, it may also be used for financial and management planning and reporting.

The ledger has a calendar of financial periods that define the time buckets into which accounting values are summarized, in both the posting and summary accounts. Each period specifies its start (or end) date, and if it is open for posting. When open, values are posted to the account period's actual value; otherwise, values are posted to its adjustment value.

A posting account has no subsidiary accounts, and so it is a leaf of a summary hierarchy and is therefore a direct measure of financial value, which allows posting accounts to be combined with the various types of entity accounts described in previous sections. For this to be practical, both the posting account and the entity account must have the same financial calendar, currency, and magnitude. This approach combines traditional accounting practices with the resource-event-actor (REA) concepts proposed by McCarthy [McCarthy 1982].

A summary account contains a list of other accounts from which its values are summarized. Values cannot be posted to a summary account in this model. The ledger may have several summary hierarchies—by account type, by cost center, by location, by organization, and so on—and allows drill down from summary to detail values.

Other Measures

Some measures of purpose are nonfinancial—sales volume, machine efficiency, labor attendance, supplier quality—and so are not

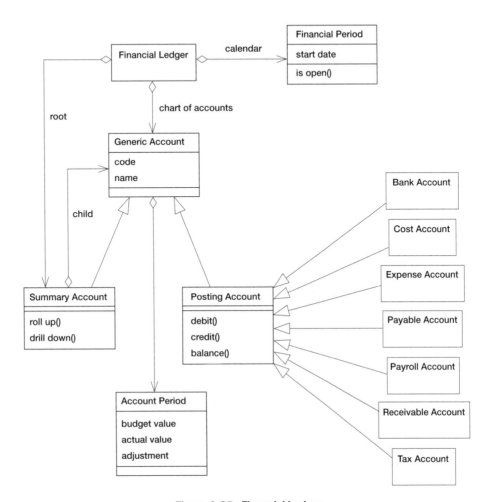

Figure A-25   Financial Ledger

tracked by ledger accounts but by other measures having similar
characteristics. A measure is typically simpler than an account
because there is no need to match and batch, or even to record, the
transactions that affect its value. Conversely, a measure typically
has a unit of measure by which to convert quantities, and its summary hierarchy may be more complex. For example, machine efficiency as a percentage might be summarized according to its
weighted average values.

Summary

The simple system does not attempt to model a real enterprise, but to demonstrate how simple, reusable components can be assembled in such a model. The reuse of classes in this model ranges from `Process Generic` (9), through `Account` (5) and `Postal Address` (3), to `Structure` (1). Naturally, these figures increase substantially as the size of the model grows. Levels of abstraction are clearly identified as:

- Organization level: relates high-level purpose, processes, and entities

- Entity level: relates an entity role to its values and other entity roles

- Process level: relates a process and its steps to entity roles and values

- Purpose level: relates process steps to measures of purpose

- Value level: defines value components such as accounts, descriptions, and so on

These levels of abstraction can be extended to suit particular requirements. The value level offers the best opportunities for reuse of model components, and entity roles can be reused for different processes within an organization. The common behavior modeled by generic entity and process components tends to be complex, and so should also be standardized and reused with minimal change. The flexibility required of practical enterprise systems is achieved through adaptable process steps and workflow and through multiple (and possibly overlapping) entity roles.

Glossary

This glossary is drawn from several sources, which are cited in the bibliography. Objects in the glossary, unless otherwise stated, mean instances of objects. Synonyms and related terms, where applicable, are listed below the description of each term.

Abstract class

A class with the purpose of being inherited by other classes [Jacobson et al. 1995].

- *Class*
- *Type*

Action

An action that takes place in the real world which is atomic from the point of view of the information system (that is, either it happens or it doesn't). This is the lowest level of decomposition of a business process.

Performs some action by invoking operations as a result of a rule firing [OMG 1998].

- *Activity*
- *Transaction*

Activity

A logical step of description of a piece of work within a process definition that contributes toward the achievement of the process [WfMC 1994].

Activity diagram

A diagram showing an activity graph that shows a procedure or a workflow [Rumbaugh et al. 1999].

- *Process*
- *Role activity diagram*

Actor

A human or mechanical resource that can do work in the context of a business process. A human actor is known as a participant. Work items are allocated to actors by the process scheduler according to rules specified in the process definition.

An actor (to a business system) defines one role or a set of roles that someone or something in the environment can play in relation to a business [Jacobson et al. 1995].

An actor (to an information system) defines one role or a set of roles that someone or something in the environment can play in relation to an information system. An example of an actor is a user of an information system [Jacobson et al. 1995].

Someone or something that can act; synonym for subject and linguistic agent [Verharen 1997].

- *Organization role*
- *Participant*
- *User*
- *Worklist*
- *Workload*

Ad hoc process

An ad hoc business process is one that is not strictly defined or is not completely specified, allowing some flexibility with respect to its use.

- *Administrative process*
- *Production process*

Administrative process

An administrative business process is one that is well defined and is adequately specified to enable some flexibility with respect to its use, while enforcing policy.

- *Ad hoc process*
- *Production process*

Agenda

The actions to be performed by an agent, instantly or at some designated point in time [Verharen 1997].

- *Action*
- *Agent*
- *Objective*
- *Schedule*

Agent

An autonomous software program to which tasks can be delegated. Software agents include mobile agents, interface agents, intelligent agents, and even entertainment agents and computer viruses.

- *Intelligent agent*
- *Organization unit*

Aggregation

An identifiable set of objects that has meaning. The aggregate itself is usually modeled as an object composed of the identifiable set of objects, each of which is considered to be part of the aggregate object [Jacobson et al. 1995].

Defines a relationship from a container type to its contents. The contents aggregates into the container but is not owned by the container [OMG 1998].

A form of association that specifies a whole-part relationship between an aggregate (a whole) and a constituent part [Rumbaugh 1999].

- *Association*
- *Composition*

Area of concern

A domain or viewpoint from which to model an aspect of a system or role of an object.

- *Domain*
- *Subject matter expert*
- *Viewpoint*

Artifact
A role of an entity that is the subject of a process.

- *Entity*
- *Role*

Association
A directed binary relation between objects. An association always links together two objects (instances or classes). It is always the associating object that acts on and knows of the associated object, never the other way around [Jacobson et al. 1995].

Attribute
A conceptual notion. An attribute of an object is an identifiable association between the object and some other entity or entities. Typically, the association is revealed by an operation with a single parameter identifying the object [OMG 1992].

Represents properties that one wishes to attach to an object [Jacobson et al. 1995].

As a property of a business object, a fact about the business object relevant to fulfilling its business purpose [OMG 1995].

A real or computed named "slot" that can hold primitive or dependent types. Attributes and relationships comprise the structural aspects of the type [OMG 1998].

- *Property*
- *Relationship*
- *State*

Automated role
Organization role that executes automatically without involving a human actor.

- *Actor*
- *Organization role*

Backflush
Assumes that the resources required to perform a process have been used when that process is completed.

Balanced scorecard
A set of measures for achieving a balance among customer expectations, internal performance, future growth, and shareholder value [Kaplan and Norton 1992].

BPR
Business process reengineering.

Business communication
The network of discrete, recurrent communicative actions that form the core of an organization. The focus is on the communication processes used to understand the business, instead of on the current organizational structures or document flows [Verharen 1997].

- *Business process*
- *Communication*
- *Organization unit*

Business engineering
The engineering of business systems to optimize resources, processes, and organization [Taylor 1995].

Business model
A business model is a model of a company that shows the company's function in the world, what it does, how, and when. It is designed to serve the needs of one or more types of handlers and it should contain the information these handlers need—no more and no less [Jacobson et al. 1995].

Business name
As a property of a business object, the term used by business experts to classify a business object [OMG 1995].

Business object
A representation of a thing that is active in the business domain, including at least its business name and definition, attributes, behavior, relationships, and constraints. A business object may represent, for example, a person, place, or concept. The representation

may be in a natural language, a modeling language, or a programming language [OMG 1995].

The supertype of all objects with identity that directly represent business concepts. Subtypes include entity, process, and subsystem [OMG 1998].

- *Business entity*
- *Business process*
- *Organization unit*

Business object document

An electronic document that defines the process interaction between business objects of different vendors. It has a labeled text format implemented across heterogeneous environments [OAG 1997].

Business process

A series of coherent activities that creates a result with some value for an external or internal customer; it is a meaningful whole of value-adding activities [Verharen 1997].

A kind of process that supports and/or is relevant to business organizational structure and policy for the purpose of achieving business objectives. This includes manual processes and/or workflow processes [WfMC 1994].

- *Activity*
- *Process*
- *Value chain*

Business system

The modeling construct we use to symbolize a business [Jacobson et al. 1995].

Capability

The list of processes that an organization is capable of performing, or a list of roles that it supports. The unit may not be able to perform the processes if it has insufficient capacity.

Capacity

The ability of a resource to perform a process step at a specific time.

- *Resource*

Class

An implementation that can be instantiated to create multiple objects with the same behavior. An object is an instance of a class. Types classify objects according to a common interface; classes classify objects according to a common implementation [OMG 1992].

Contains a definition that all objects belonging to the class can follow [Jacobson et al. 1995].

- *Interface*
- *Type*

Collection

A type that contains references to sets of other instances, parameterized by the type contained in the collection, which are one of the following [OMG 1998]:

Set: unordered collection without duplicates

List: ordered collection allowing duplicates

Ulist: ordered collection without duplicates

Bag: unordered collection allowing duplicates

Array: indexed collection allowing duplicates

Iterator: transient index for iterating through a collection, based on a selection criterion

Extent: set of all instances of a particular type

Home: subset of extent

Communication

Coordination of activities by exchanging messages; its essence is to commit the partners in communication to a course of action so that one can rely on the other [Verharen 1997].

- *Action*
- *Message*

Composition

A form of aggregation association with strong ownership and coincident lifetime of parts by the whole [Rumbaugh et al. 1999].

- *Aggregation*
- *Association*

Compound process

A process that has more than one step, typically constrained by workflow rules.

- *Process*
- *Workflow*

Constraint

Applied to proposed changes in single or multivalued attributes and relationships to determine if they may be effected [OMG 1998].

Contract

Specifies the stimuli that can be communicated between two instances of two different classes [Jacobson et al. 1995].

The presence of a precondition and a postcondition in a routine should be viewed as a contract that binds the routine and its callers [Meyer 1988].

A set of mutually agreed upon obligations and related authorizations between different parties about services provided to each other, together with rules governing violation. It describes the effect of transactions [Verharen 1997].

A contract is a unit of cooperation between two or more organization units.

A legal contract setting out the requirements and responsibilities of business partners who exchange electronic data.

- *Organization unit*
- *Party*
- *Transaction*
- *Violation*

CORBA

Common Object Request Broker Architecture.

Customer

Role of an entity that uses products and services downstream in a value network or supply chain.

Party to a contract.

- *Contract*
- *Party*
- *Supply chain*
- *Value network*

Data warehouse

A multidimensional representation of an enterprise, typically including axes for values, locations, organization, and time.

- *Information*
- *Purpose*

Deadline

The time by which an action should be performed, or a particular state should be reached [Verharen 1997].

- *Action*

Delegation

Transfer or assignment of authorization, obligations, and controls to a subordinate actor [Verharen 1997].

- *Actor*
- *Authorization*
- *Obligation*

Deontic logic

Study of ethics and moral obligations.

Logic to reason about obligations and authorizations [Verharen 1997].

- *Obligation*
- *Purpose*

Deliverable

An output from a process that has a value—material or abstract—for a customer [Jacobson et al. 1995].

- *Purpose*

Document

An input or output document that is used in a business and is the primary interface between a business system and a person.

Domain

An area of business or other form of activity that shares common attributes and processes.

- *Area of concern*
- *Subject matter expert*
- *Viewpoint*

Downstream

The direction in which materials flow in a supply chain. A customer is downstream from its suppliers.

- *Customer*
- *Performer*
- *Supply chain*

Economic value added

Measures that capture the true value of an enterprise over time [Stern 1996].

EDI
Electronic data interchange.

EDIFACT
EDI for Administration, Commerce, and Transport is an international standard that includes the rules of EDI application, implementation, and message design. It is developed and maintained under the auspices of the UN.

Electronic data interchange
The electronic transfer of information structured according to common standards, from one computer application to another application.

Encapsulation
The only visible part of an object is the services that are offered, not how they are performed. The information contained in an object, and how the operations are performed, are not visible from outside the object [Jacobson et al. 1995].

Entity
A business object that represents a business noun or actor. A business entity object is a specialization (type) of business object [OMG 1995].

The primary object for storing the values of a business.

An object (in a business system) that represents occurrences such as products, deliverables, documents, and other things that are handled in the business [Jacobson et al. 1995].

An object (in an information system) that manages some piece of information or some resource and its access [Jacobson et al. 1995].

The most common type of business object, representing people, places, things, and companies that are persistent, transactional, secure, and identifiable [OMG 1998].

- *Business object*
- *Resource*

Event
Persistent business objects designed to record a significant event in the life of the business [OMG 1998].

Changes to or within an object are events in its lifetime.

- *Process*

Exception
Represent problems within an invocation or transaction [OMG 1998].

Facade
A facade is a single object through which all communication to a component flows [D'Souza and Wills 1999].

Flowchart
A diagram that represents a sequence of events, usually drawn with standard symbols.

- *Activity diagram*

Forward engineering
Describes the new business processes [Jacobson et al. 1995].

- *Reengineering*
- *Reverse engineering*

Generalization
The inverse of the specialization relation [OMG 1992].

Goods
A tangible product that is typically manufactured, shipped, and held in inventory prior to sale or use.

- *Product*
- *Service*

Hierarchy of purpose
The hierarchical relationship among vision, mission, goals, and objectives [Enterprise 1995].

- *Objective*
- *Purpose*

Information

Results derived from processing of data so as to provide knowledge and increase understanding [Sander 1997]. Information is degraded by noise.

- *Noise*

Information system

A software system used to support the activities in a business [Jacobson et al. 1995].

- *Information*

Inheritance

The construction of a definition by incremental modification of the other definitions [OMG 1991].

Intelligent agent

A software program that has autonomy, social ability, reactivity, and proactiveness; and knowledge, beliefs, intentions, and obligations with which to reason and make decisions.

- *Agent*
- *Organization unit*

Interaction diagram

A diagram that shows how a use-case is realized by communicating objects [Jacobson et al. 1995].

Interface

A listing of operations and attributes that an object provides. This includes the signatures of the operation and the types of the attributes. An interface definition ideally includes the semantics as well. An object satisfies an interface if it can be specified as the target object in each potential request described by the interface [OMG 1991].

A shared boundary across which information is passed; a [software] component that connects two or more other components for the purpose of passing information from one to the other [CMU/SEI-93-TR-23].

- *Class*
- *Type*

Invariant

A condition that must be satisfied by all instances of a type, which may hold all the time, when a given trigger causes an event notification, or deferred with a schedule [OMG 1998].

A constraint that must be true at all times (or, at least, at all times when no operation is incomplete) [Rumbaugh et al. 1999].

- *Postcondition*
- *Precondition*

ISO

International Standards Organization.

ISO 9000

The set of ISO standards by which the quality of the design and delivery of products and services is defined and managed [ISO 9000-1 1994].

IT

Information technology.

Iteration

A workflow process activity cycle involving the repetitive execution of workflow process activity(or activities) until a condition is met [WfMC 1994].

- *Workflow loop*

Join

When two or more parallel executing activities converge into a single common thread of control [WfMC 1994].

The UML activity diagram uses the term "synchronize" to describe a join [Rumbaugh et al. 1999].

- *Split*

Kanban

An artifact such as a bin or card that indicates the need for, or availability of, inventory in a manufacturing process.

Lead time

The period of time between the ordering of a product by a customer from a supplier and its receipt by the customer.

Legacy system

An existing computer system that contains data and/or applications that are of value to an organization.

Lexicon

The system that stores and manages the terminology of a certain domain [Verharen 1997].

- *Ontology*

Master schedule

An authoritative statement of how many (product) end items are to be produced and when [Orlicky 1975].

- *Plan*

Materials planning

Material requirements or material procurement planning to calculate the future quantities of materials and components that are required.

- *Planning*

Message

A speech act that describes the illocutionary force, or speaker's intentions, together with its authorization claim and its content [Verharen 1997].

A message (in an EDI context) is the collection of data, organized in segments, exchanged to convey business transactions between partners engaged in EDI. Also called a document or transaction set.

- *Speech act*

Metamodel

A model that defines the language for expressing a model [Rumbaugh et al. 1999].

- *Model*

Method

An implementation of an operation. Code that may be executed to perform a requested service. Methods associated with an object may be structured into one or more programs [OMG 1991].

Milestone

A kind of purpose often used in project environments.

- *Objective*
- *Purpose*
- *Work breakdown structure*

Model

A semantically complete abstraction of a system [Rumbaugh et al. 1999].

- *Metamodel*

Multiple inheritance

The construction of a definition by incremental modification of more than one other definition [OMG 1991].

The inheritance by a class of properties from several other classes [Jacobson et al. 1995].

- *Inheritance*

Noise

Spurious or unnecessary data that degrades the quality of information.

- *Information*

Non-value-adding

The activities in a business process that do not give anything of value to a customer. The opposite of value-adding activities [Jacobson et al. 1995].

- *Value-adding*
- *Value network*

Object

A combination of a state and a set of methods that explicitly embodies an abstraction characterized by the behavior of the relevant requests. An object is an instance of an implementation and an interface. An object models a real-world entity, and it is implemented as a computational entity that encapsulates state and operations (internally implemented as data and methods) and responds to requester services [OMG 1991].

An identifiable, encapsulated entity that provides one or more services that can be requested [Jacobson et al. 1995].

Object name

A value that identifies an object [OMG 1992].

Object reference

A value that unambiguously identifies an object. An object reference is never reused to identify another object [OMG 1992].

Object request broker

Provides the means by which clients make and receive requests and responses [OMG 1992].

Objective

A desired future value of an entity. The lowest level, or leaf node, of a purpose hierarchy.

- *Purpose hierarchy*

Obligation

Something that must be fulfilled, done, or brought about. An obligation is the result of a commitment of an actor, or of a command by an actor having a power relationship, or of a request by an actor that is given authority [Verharen 1997].

- *Actor*
- *Agenda*
- *Organization unit*

Ontology

The features of a conceptual model used to structure and describe knowledge of a domain.

- *Domain*
- *Lexicon*

Operation

A service that can be requested. An operation has an association signature (protocol) that may restrict the actual parameters that are possible in a meaningful request [OMG 1992].

One identifiable entity that denotes a service that can be requested by an object definition [Jacobson et al. 1995].

Extends OMG 1992 definition with feature parameters, preconditions, postconditions, event production, and computed values [OMG 1998].

- *Interface*
- *Method*
- *Request*

ORB

Object request broker.

Organization role

A viewpoint from which to define process steps and entity roles.

- *Entity*
- *Organizational unit*
- *Process*

Organization (unit)

Manages a group of entities that perform business processes in order to achieve purpose.

- *Intelligent agent*
- *Organization role*
- *Process*
- *Purpose*

Participant

A participant is a real human actor who performs work, typically within the context of business processes.

A resource that performs some or all of the work represented by a workflow process activity instance [WfMC 1994].

- *Actor*
- *User*

Party

An individual or corporate entity involved in a contract or process.

- *Customer*
- *Perfomer*

Performer

A role of an entity able to supply products or services, which is upstream in a value network or chain.

A party to a contract.

- *Contract*
- *Party*

Permission

The allowance of the commitment to and/or operation of an action [Verharen 1997].

- *Action*

Persistent object

An object that can survive the process or thread that created it. A persistent object exists until it is explicitly deleted [OMG 1991].

- *Transient object*

Plan

A statement of objectives, typically ordered in sequence of due date or priority.

- *Objective*
- *Planning*
- *Purpose*
- *Schedule*

Planning

A business process for creating and maintaining a plan.

- *Plan*

Policy

A course of action adopted in a situation.

- *Situation*

Power

Power relationships are defined by the hierarchical structure of authority between agents or organization units [Verharen 1997].

- *Agent*
- *Contract*
- *Organization unit*

Postcondition

A constraint that must be true at the completion of an operation [Rumbaugh et al. 1999].

- *Invariant*
- *Precondition*

Precedence

A constraining relation between activities.

Precondition

A constraint that must be true when an operation is invoked [Rumbaugh et al. 1999].

- *Invariant*
- *Postcondition*

Presentation

Services required in order to display objects to human actors or participants.

Process

A coordinated (parallel and/or serial) set of activities that are connected in order to achieve a common goal. A process activity may be a manual activity and/or a workflow process activity [WfMC 1994].

A set of partially ordered steps intended to reach a goal. A process is decomposable into process steps and process components. The former represent the smallest, atomic level; the latter may range from individual process steps to very large parts of processes [CMU/SEI-93-TR-23].

- *Activity*
- *Process definition*
- *Transaction*

Process definition

The computerized representation or model of a process that defines both the manual process and the automated workflow process [WfMC 1994].

- *Process instance*

Process handbook

An electronic document detailing best work practices in several different companies [Malone et al. 1997].

Process instance
An instance of a process definition that includes the manual and automated workflow processes [WfMC 1994].

- *Process definition*

Process leader
The individual who is responsible for an instance of a process, and who may in many ways be similar to a project leader [Jacobson et al. 1995].

Process monitoring
The tracking of events during process execution [WfMC 1994].

Process operator
Process operators are the individuals working to perform a process. Each individual may take part in one or several business processes [Jacobson et al. 1995].

Process owner
The individual who is responsible for a process in a business. This responsibility entails defining the process, determining the interface of the process, defining goals of the process, planning the budget, appointing process leaders, allocating resources, and developing the process itself [Jacobson et al. 1995].

Process role
A synergistic collection of workflow process activities that can be assumed and performed by a workflow participant for the purpose of achieving process objectives [WfMC 1994].

- *Organization role*

Process step
A logical step or description of a piece of work that contributes toward the accomplishment of a process. A process activity may be a manual process activity and/or an automated workflow process activity [WfMC 1994].

Product

An artifact that is bought and sold, including standard, custom, and configurable goods and services.

- *Goods*
- *Service*

Production planning

Calculation of the future quantity to produce, based on customer orders, demand forecasts, inventory levels in the supply chain, and production capacities.

- *Master schedule*
- *Planning*

Production process

A production business process is one that is strictly defined and is completely specified, allowing little or no flexibility with respect to its use.

- *Ad hoc process*
- *Administrative process*

Project

A type of business process, typically having a single purpose.

- *Milestone*
- *Process*
- *Work breakdown structure*

Property

A conceptual notion. An attribute, the value of which can be changed [OMG 1992].

Purpose

A state of affairs that an organization intends to achieve. Organizational units hold one or more purposes, and business processes are designed to achieve purposes. Specialized purposes include, in order of decreasing complexity and duration, vision, missions, goals, and objectives [Enterprise 1995].

- *Hierarchy of purpose*
- *Organizational unit*
- *Process*

Reengineering

Reverse engineering of an existing process followed by forward engineering of a new process [Jacobson et al. 1995].

- *Forward engineering*
- *Reverse engineering*

Relationship

An association between objects.

As a property of a business object, an association between business objects that reflects the interaction of their business purposes [OMG 1995].

A semantic connection between types, the basis for connecting business objects into a framework for a specific purpose [OMG 1998].

- *Business object*

Release

The enactment of a process designed to achieve an objective.

- *Objective*
- *Process*

Request

A client issues a request to cause a service to be performed. A request consists of an operation and zero or more actual parameters [OMG 1991].

An event consisting of an operation and zero or more actual parameters. A client issues a request to cause a service to be performed. Also associated with a request are the results that may be returned to the client. A message can be used to implement (carry) a request and/or result [OMG 1992].

- *Interface*
- *Operation*

Requirements analysis

Analysis performed in order to develop a requirements model, including a use-can model, of an information system [Jacobson et al. 1995].

Requirements capturing

Gathering of the necessary information needed in order to build a requirements model [Jacobson et al. 1995].

Resource

The role of an entity that models capacity to be used and produced by business processes. The capacity may be consumed, incorporated, monopolized, or accessed [Taylor 1995].

- *Capacity*

Resource owner

The individual who owns the resources in a business. This responsibility means making sure that all individuals are allocated somewhere, solving resource conflicts, establishing development plans for each individual, and also taking care of recruitment [Jacobson et al. 1995].

Results

The information returned to the client, which may include values as well as status information indicating that exceptional conditions were raised in attempting to perform the requested service [OMG 1991].

Reverse engineering

Development of an abstract model of an existing business and its processes. This encompasses a variety of activities with the objective of gaining understanding of the business, and also communicating this understanding [Jacobson et al. 1995].

- *Forward engineering*
- *Reengineering*

Risk

The probability or chance of an objective not being met, sometimes measurable by statistical techniques.

- *Objective*
- *Value*

Role

A synergistic collection of defined attributes, qualifications, and/or skills that can be assumed and performed by a workflow participant for the purpose of achieving organizational objectives [WfMC 1994].

An optional, specialized view of an entity for a particular model. Roles are dynamic sub-types and may be added to or removed from the entity at any time.

- *Actor*
- *Entity*
- *Organizational role*

Role activity diagram

An activity diagram divided into swimlanes that represent organization roles [Ould 1995].

- *Activity diagram*

Rule

As a property of a business object, a constraint which governs the behavior, relationships, and attributes of a business object [OMG 1995].

Scenario

A set of actions that represents one of many possible ways in which a process can be enacted, or in which an organization can develop.

Schedule

A set of objectives, typically listed in order of due date or priority.

- *Agenda*
- *Objective*
- *Plan*

Service

An intangible product, typically rendered by a business process.

- *Goods*
- *Product*

Simulation

The ability to simulate the consequence of the execution or occurrence of a set of actions on a business model.

Situation

The states or values of one or more purposes, processes, or entities, also known as a state of affairs.

- *State*
- *Value*

Speech act

An utterance or message with a performative nature; what one is doing in saying something [Verharen 1997].

- *Message*

Split

The decision of a single thread of control among multiple parallel process activities [WfMC 1994].

The UML activity diagram uses the term fork to describe a split [Rumbaugh et al. 1999].

- *Join*

State

The time varying properties of an object that affects the object's behavior [OMG 1991].

A state tells one where an object is in its life cycle, and what events can make it change to a new state [Jacobson et al. 1995].

State transition diagram

A diagram showing the states and the transitions that an object may pass through during its lifetime [Jacobson et al. 1995].

State transition rule

A rule that specifies the conditions under which an object goes from one state to another, defining a trigger, a condition, when the rule should fire, the initial (source) and the final (target) states [OMG 1998].

STD

State transition diagram.

Stereotype

A new kind of model element within the model based on an existing kind of model element [Rumbaugh et al. 1999].

- *Class*
- *Object*

Strategic purpose

A strategic purpose is one that is declared to be of strategic importance, typically a vision or mission. Higher-level purposes are also strategic [Enterprise 1995].

- *Purpose*
- *Strategy*

Strategy

A strategy is a business process designed to achieve a strategic purpose [Enterprise 1995].

- *Process*
- *Purpose*
- *Strategic purpose*

Subject matter expert

A person who understands the business requirements in a specific domain [Kilov 1999].

- *Area of concern*
- *Domain*
- *User*

Supply chain

A set of organization units that cooperate to deliver goods from supplier to customers.

- *Downstream*
- *Organization unit*
- *Upstream*
- *Value network*

Transaction

A logical grouping of speech acts with temporal constraints between them, including an optional deadline [Verharen 1997].

- *Action*
- *Business process*
- *Deadline*
- *Speech act*

Type

A predicate (Boolean function) defined over values that can be used in a signature to restrict a possible parameter or characterize a possible result. Types classify objects according to a common interface; classes classify objects according to a common implementation [OMG 1992].

A class or definition of an object. Types are arranged into a type hierarchy that forms a directed cyclic graph [OMG 1995].

- *Class*
- *Interface*

Unit of work

An atomic process step, which may or may not achieve a separate objective.

A set of changes that are committed or rolled back as one [Sims 1994].

- *Objective*
- *Process step*
- *Work*

Upstream

The direction in a supply chain opposite to the flow of materials. A supplier is upstream of its customer.

- *Customer*
- *Performer*
- *Supply chain*

Use case

A sequence of transactions (in a business system) whose task is to yield a result of measurable value to an individual actor of the business system [Jacobson et al. 1995].

A behaviorally related sequence of transactions (in an information system) performed by an actor in a dialogue with the system to provide some measurable value to the actor [Jacobson et al. 1995].

- *Business process*
- *Scenario*

User

A person who is assigned certain organization roles in relation to an information system. Rights are allocated to roles, and users gain rights by virtue of their roles.

- *Actor*
- *Role*

User interface

Means by which a user interacts with a process.

- *Document*
- *Process*

Value

Any entity that may be a possible actual parameter in a request. Values that serve to identify objects are called object references [OMG 1991].

The value of a business entity and the value added by a business process are increased by addition of monetary value and by reduction of associated risk.

- *Risk*

Value-adding

Any activity in a business process that, from the customer's perspective, increases the value of the final product [Jacobson et al. 1995].

- *Non-value-adding*
- *Value*

Value driver

The hierarchical relationship between a value at a higher level and those values at a lower level from which it is derived [Nickols 1997].

- *Hierarchy of purpose*
- *Value*

Value network

A network or chain of organization units formed to deliver value.

- *Organization unit*
- *Value*

Viewpoint

A form of abstraction achieved using a selected set of architectural concepts and structuring rules, in order to focus on particular concerns within a system [ISO/IEC 10746 1995].

- *Area of concern*
- *Domain*
- *Subject matter expert*

Violation

Violation is failing to adhere to obligations, which causes sanctions described in the contract to be invoked, and subtasks to be rescheduled.

- *Contract*
- *Obligation*

WIP

Work in process.

Work

Performance of an activity as part of a business process.

- *Activity*
- *Process step*
- *Unit of work*
- *Work item*

Work breakdown structure

A kind of hierarchy of purpose often used in project environments.

- *Hierarchy of purpose*
- *Purpose*

Work in process

A nonatomic process that has started but is not yet complete.

- *Process*

Work item

Representation of work to be processed in the context of a workflow process activity in a workflow process instance. Work items are assigned to and performed by participants by means of documents and applications [WfMC 1994].

Workflow

The computerized facilitation or automated component of a process [WfMC 1994].

Workflow activity

The computer automation of a logical step that contributes toward the completion of a process [WfMC 1994].

- *Activity*
- *Process step*

Workflow loop

A molecular element of a business process; an interaction between two people in which one—the performer—fulfills a commitment to the satisfaction of the other—the customer [White and Fischer 1994].

- *Customer*
- *Performer*
- *Process*

Worklist

A list of all work items accessible to an actor (human or mechanical), typically ordered in priority sequence. Work items are allocated to a worklist by the process scheduler to balance workloads and to minimize queue length.

- *Actor*
- *Participant*
- *Work item*
- *Workload*
- *Workpool*

Workload

The capacity (typically time) required of an actor to do the work in the worklist. The workload is used by the process scheduler to allocate work items to worklists to best satisfy the process objectives.

- *Actor*
- *Participant*
- *Work item*
- *Worklist*

Workpool

A list of all work items accessible to an organization role, typically ordered in priority sequence. Work items are allocated to the workpool based on the user role(s) specified for the activity in the process definition.

- *Work item*
- *Worklist*

Bibliography

[Balasubramanian and Norrie 1996] Sivaram Balasubramanian and Douglas H. Norrie, *A Multi-Agent Intelligent Design System Integrating Manufacturing and Shop-Floor Control.* University of Calgary: Department of Mechanical Engineering, 1996.

[Bigus and Bigus 1998] Joseph P. Bigus and Jennifer Bigus. *Constructing Intelligent Agents with Java: A Programmer's Guide to Smarter Applications.* John Wiley & Sons, 1998.

[Booch 1994] Grady Booch, *Object-Oriented Analysis and Design with Applications, Second Edition,* Addison–Wesley Longman, 1994.

[Breu et al. 1997] Ruth Breu, Radu Grosu, Christof Hofmann, Franz Huber, Ingolf Kruger, Bernhard Rumpe, Monica Schmidt, and Wolfgang Schwerin, *Exemplary and Complete Object Interaction Descriptions,* OOPSLA'97 Workshop on Object-Oriented Behavioral Semantics, 1997.

[Breuner 1995] Emily F. Breuner, *Complexity and Organization Structure: Internet and Visa International as Prototypes for the Corporation of the Future.* MIT Sloane School of Management, 1995.

[Brynjolfsson et al. 1993] Erik Brynjolfsson, Thomas W. Malone, Vijay Gurbaxani and Ajit Kambil, *An Empirical Analysis of the Relationship Between Information Technology and Firm Size,* Center for Coordination Science, MIT, 1993.

[Checkland 1981] Peter Checkland. *Systems Thinking, Systems Practice,* John Wiley & Sons, 1981.

[Clausewitz 1984] Carl von Clausewitz: translated by Michael Howard and Peter Paret, *On War,* Princeton University Press, 1984.

[CMU/SEI-93-TR-23] Alan Brown et al., *Reference Model for Project Support Environments (Version 2.0),* Carnegie-Mellon University: Software Engineering Institute, 1993.

[Creveld 1985] Martin van Creveld, *Command in War,* Harvard University Press, 1985.

[Dignum and Weigand 1994] Frank Dignum and Hans Weigand, *Communication and Deontic Logic: Proceedings ISCORE '94 Workshop,* Vrije Universiteit: Amsterdam, 1994.

[D'Souza and Wills 1999] Desmond D'Souza and Alan Cameron Wills. *Objects, Components, and Frameworks with UML: The Catalysis Approach,* Addison-Wesley Longman, 1999.

[Ehrbar 1998] Al Ehrbar, *EVA: The Real Key to Creating Wealth,* John Wiley & Sons, 1998.

[Enterprise 1995] The Enterprise Project, Ontology ENTERPRISE-V0.1, AIAI, 1995.

[Fowler 1997] Martin Fowler. *Analysis Patterns: Reusable Object Models,* Addison–Wesley Longman, 1997.

[Fowler 1997A] Martin Fowler, *Dealing with Roles, Supplement for Analysis Patterns: Reusable Object Models,* Addison–Wesley Longman,1997.

[Goldratt 1992] Eliyahu M. Goldratt and Jeff Cox. *The Goal: A Process of Ongoing Improvement,* North River Press, 1992.

[Hammer and Champy 1993] Michael Hammer and James Champy, *Reengineering the Corporation: A Manifesto for Business Revolution.* Nicholas Brealey Publishing Ltd, 1993.

[Howard 1996] David Howard, *Discussion on Roles,* BPR List, 1996.

[ISO 9000-1 1994] International Standards Organization, Quality Management and Quality Assurance Standards, ISO, 1994.

[ISO 10303 1994] International Standards Organization, Product Data Interchange using STEP, ISO, 1994.

[ISO/IEC 10746 1995] International Standards Organization, ODP Reference Model, ISO, 1995.

[Jacobson et al. 1995] Ivar Jacobson, Maria Ericsson and Agneta Jacobson, *The Object Advantage: Business Process Reengineering with Object Technology,* Addison–Wesley Longman, 1995.

[Jacobson et al. 1999] Ivar Jacobson, Grady Booch and James Rumbaugh, *The Unified Software Development Process,* Addison–Wesley Longman, 1999.

[Jaques 1989] Elliott Jaques, *Requisite Organization :the CEO's Guide to Creative Structure and Leadership,* Cason Hall and Co, 1989.

[Jayashankar et al. 1996] Swaminathan M. Jayashankar, Norman M. Sadeh and Stephen F. Smith, *Information Exchange in the Supply Chain,* The Robotics Institute: Carnegie Mellon University, 1996.

[Kaplan and Norton 1992] Robert S. Kaplan and David P. Norton, *The Balanced Scorecard: Measures that Drive Performance,* Harvard Business Review, 1992.

[Kelly 1994] Kevin Kelly, *Out of Control: The New Biology of Machines, Social Systems, and the Economic World,* Addison-Wesley, 1994.

[Kilov 1999] Haim Kilov, *Business Specifications: The Key to Successful Software Engineering,* Prentice Hall, 1999.

[Laubacher and Malone 1997] Robert J. Laubacher and Thomas W. Malone, *Flexible Work Arrangements and 21st Century Worker's Guilds,* MIT Sloane School of Management Working Paper 21C WP #004, 1997.

[Laubacher et al. 1997] Robert J. Laubacher, Thomas W. Malone , and the MIT Scenario Working Group, *Two Scenarios for 21st Century Organizations: Shifting Networks of Small Firms or All-Encompassing "Virtual Countries"?,* MIT Sloane School of Management Working Paper 21C WP #001, 1997.

[Malone et al. 1997] Thomas W. Malone, Kevin Crowston, Jintae Lee, Brian Pentland, Chrysanthos Dellarocas, George Wyner, John Quimby, Charley Osborne and Abraham Bernstein, *Tools for Inventing Organizations: Towards a Handbook of Organizational Processes,* MIT Center for Coordination Science, 1997.

[Matthews 1996] Mike Matthews, *An Agent-Based Framework for Integrated Intelligent Planning-Execution,* Advanced Technology Program, National Institute of Standards and Technology, 1996.

[McCarthy 1982] William E. McCarthy, *The REA Accounting Model: A Generalized Framework for Accounting Systems in a Shared Data Environment,* The Accounting Review Vol. LVII, No. 3, July 1982.

[Meyer 1988] Bertrand Meyer, *Object-Oriented Software Construction,* Prentice-Hall, 1988.

[Miles and Snow 1978] Raymond E. Miles and Charles C. Snow, *Organizational Strategy, Structure, and Process,* McGraw-Hill, 1978.

[Minar et al. 1996] Nelson Minar, Roger Burkhart, Chris Langton and Manor Askenazi, *The Swarm Simulation System:A Toolkit for Building Multi-agent Simulations,* Santa Fe Institute, 1996.

[Mintzberg 1979] Henry Mintzberg, *The Structuring of Organizations,* Prentice-Hall, 1979.

[Moncrieff and Smallwood 1997] James Moncrieff and Janet Smallwood, *Ideas for the New Millenium. FT Mastering,* Pearson Professional, 1997.

[Nickols 1997] Fred Nickols, *Measurement Based Analysis: Hooking what You Do to The Bottom Line,* The Distance Consulting Company, 1997.

[OMG 1991] Object Management Group, *The Common Object Request Broker: Architecture and Specification,* Object Management Group, 1991.

[OMG 1992] Object Management Group, *Object Management Architecture Guide,* Object Management Group, 1992.

[OMG 1995] Object Management Group, *BOMSIG White Paper,* OMG, 1995.

[OMG 1997] Object Management Group, *V-ERP White Paper/Roadmap,* OMG, 1997.

[OMG 1998] Object Management Group, *Organizational Structure Facility,* OMG, 1998.

[Orlicky 1975] Joseph Orlicky, *Material Requirements Planning: the New Way of Life in Production and Inventory Management,* McGraw-Hill, 1975.

[Ould 1995] Martyn A. Ould, *Business Processes: Modelling and Analysis for Re-engineering and Improvement,* John Wiley & Sons, 1995.

[Reenskaug 1996] Trygve Reenskaug, *Working with Objects: The OOram Software Engineering Method.* Greenwich, CT: Manning Publications, 1996.

[Robbins 1990] Stephen P. Robbins, *Organization Theory: Structure, Design and Applications,* Prentice-Hall, 1990.

[Rosenberg 1999] Doug Rosenberg with Kendall Scott. *Use Case Driven Object Modeling with UML: A Pracatical Approach.* Addison–Wesley Longman, 1999.

[Rumbaugh et al. 1999] James Rumbaugh, Ivar Jacobson and Grady Booch. *The Unified Modeling Language Reference Manual,* Addison–Wesley Longman, 1999.

[Saaty 1990] Thomas L. Saaty, *Multicriteria Decision Making: The Analytic Hierarchy Process* RWS Publications, 1990.

[Sander 1997] Emile Sander, *Marine Corps Intelligence and Security Doctrine: Command and Control,* U.S. Marine Corps, 1997.

[Schneider and Winters 1998] Geri Schneider and Jason P. Winters, *Applying Use Cases: A Practical Approach,* Addison-Wesley, 1998.

[Schonberger 1982] Richard J Schonberger, *Japanese Manufacturing Techniques: Nine Hidden Lessons in Simplicity,* Free Press, 1982.

[Senge 1990] Peter M. Senge, *The Fifth Discipline: The Art & Practice of the Learning Organization,* Doubleday Currency, 1990.

[Sims 1994] Oliver Sims, *Business Objects: Delivering Cooperative Objects for Client-Server,* McGraw-Hill, 1994.

[Sun 1997] Sun Microsystems, *Java Code Conventions,* Sun Microsystems Inc., 1995-1997.

[Taylor 1995] David A. Taylor, *Business Engineering with Object Technology,* John Wiley & Sons, 1995.

[Teigen 1997] Rune Teigen, *Information Flow in a Supply Chain Management System,* Enterprise Integration Laboratory: University of Toronto, 1997.

[UML 1997] Rational Software et al., *UML Extension for Objectory Process for Software Engineering,* OMG, 1997.

[Verharen 1997] Egon M. Verharen, *A Language-Action Perspective on the Design of Cooperative Information Agents,* The Infolab, Tilburg University, 1997.

[W3C 1997] World Wide Web Consortium, *Extensible Markup Language (XML),* W3C, 1997.

[White and Fischer 1994] Thomas E. White and Layna Fischer, *New Tools for New Times: The Workflow Paradigm.* Lighthouse Point, FL: Future Strategies, 1994.

[WfMC 1994] Workflow Management Coalition, *Glossary: A Workflow Management Coalition Specification,* Workflow Management Coalition, November 1994.

[WfMC 1995] Workflow Management Coalition, *The Workflow Reference Model,* Workflow Management Coalition, March 1995.

Index

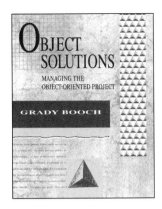

Object Solutions
Managing the Object-Oriented Project
Grady Booch
Addison-Wesley Object Technology Series

Object Solutions is a direct outgrowth of Grady Booch's experience with object-oriented projects in development around the world. This book focuses on the development process and is the perfect resource for developers and managers who want to implement object technologies for the first time or refine their existing object-oriented development practice. Drawing upon his knowledge of strategies used in both successful and unsuccessful projects, the author offers pragmatic advice for applying object technologies and controlling projects effectively.

0-8053-0594-7 • Paperback • 336 pages • ©1996

The Unified Modeling Language User Guide
Grady Booch, James Rumbaugh, and Ivar Jacobson
Addison-Wesley Object Technology Series

The Unified Modeling Language User Guide is a two-color introduction to the core eighty percent of the Unified Modeling Language, approaching it in a layered fashion and showing the application of the UML to modeling problems across a wide variety of application domains. This landmark book is suitable for developers unfamiliar with the UML or modeling in general, and will also be useful to experienced developers who wish to learn how to apply the UML to advanced problems.

0-201-57168-4 • Hardcover • 512 pages • ©1999

Surviving Object-Oriented Projects
A Manager's Guide
Alistair Cockburn
Addison-Wesley Object Technology Series

This book allows you to survive and ultimately succeed with an object-oriented project. Alistair Cockburn draws on his personal experience and extensive knowledge to provide the information that managers need to combat the unforeseen challenges that await them during project implemen-tation. Independent of language or programming environment, the book supports its key points through short case studies taken from real object-oriented projects, and an appendix collects these guidelines and solutions into brief "crib sheets"—ideal for handy reference.

0-201-49834-0 • Paperback • 272 pages • ©1998

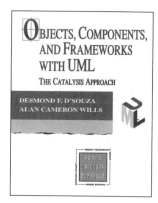

Objects, Components, and Frameworks with UML
The Catalysis^SM *Approach*
Desmond Francis D'Souza and Alan Cameron Wills
Addison-Wesley Object Technology Series

Catalysis is a rapidly emerging UML-based method for component and framework-based development with objects. The authors describe a unique UML-based approach to precise specification of component interfaces using a type model, enabling precise external description of behavior without constraining implementations. This approach provides application developers and system architects with well-defined and reusable techniques that help them build open distributed object systems from components and frameworks.

0-201-31012-0 • Paperback • 816 pages • ©1999

Doing Hard Time
Developing Real-Time Systems with UML, Objects, Frameworks, and Patterns
Bruce Powel Douglass
Addison-Wesley Object Technology Series

Doing Hard Time is written to facilitate the daunting process of developing real-time systems. The author presents an embedded systems programming methodology that has been proven successful in practice. The process outlined in this book allows application developers to apply practical techniques—garnered from the mainstream areas of object-oriented software development—to meet the demanding qualifications of real-time programming.

0-201-49837-5 • Hardcover with CD-ROM • 800 pages • ©1999

Real-Time UML, Second Edition
Developing Efficient Objects for Embedded Systems
Bruce Powel Douglass
Addison-Wesley Object Technology Series

The Unified Modeling Language is particularly suited to modeling real-time and embedded systems. *Real-Time UML, Second Edition*, is the completely updated and UML 1.3–compliant introduction that developers of real-time systems need to make the transition to object-oriented analysis and design with UML. The book covers the important features of the UML, and shows how to effectively use these features to model real-time systems. Special in-depth discussions of finite state machines, object identification strategies, and real-time design patterns to help beginning and experienced developers alike are also included.

0-201-65784-8 • Paperback • 384 pages • ©2000

UML Distilled, Second Edition

A Brief Guide to the Standard Object Modeling Language
Martin Fowler, with Kendall Scott
Addison-Wesley Object Technology Series

Thoroughly revised and updated, this best-selling book is a concise overview that introduces you to the Unified Modeling Language, highlighting the key elements of the standard modeling language's notation, semantics, and processes. Included is a brief explanation of UML's history, development, and rationale, as well as discussions on how UML can be integrated into the object-oriented development process. The book also profiles various modeling techniques associated with UML—use cases, CRC cards, design by contract, dynamic classification, interfaces, and abstract classes. The first edition of this classic work received *Software Development* magazine's 1997 Productivity Award.

0-201-65783-X • Paperback • 224 pages • ©2000

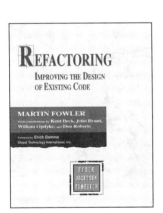

Refactoring

Improving the Design of Existing Code
Martin Fowler, with contributions by Kent Beck, John Brant, William Opdyke, and Don Roberts
Addison-Wesley Object Technology Series

Refactoring is the process of changing a software system in such a way that it does not alter the external behavior of the code, yet improves its external structure. In this book, Martin Fowler, Kent Beck, John Brant, William Opdyke, and Don Roberts show you where opportunities for refactoring can typically be found, and how to go about reworking a bad design into a good one. In addition to discussing the various techniques of refactoring, the authors provide a detailed catalog of more than seventy proven refactorings.

0-201-48567-2 • Hardcover • 464 pages • ©1999

Applied Software Architecture

Christine Hofmeister, Robert Nord, and Dilip Soni
Addison-Wesley Object Technology Series

Applied Software Architecture provides practical guidelines and techniques for producing quality software designs. The authors give an extensive overview of software architecture basics and a detailed guide to architecture design tasks, focusing on four fundamental views of architecture—conceptual, module, execution, and code. This book reveals the insights and best practices of the most skilled software architects in designing software architecture, and presents these through four real-life case studies.

0-201-32571-3 • Hardcover • 432 pages • ©2000

The Unified Software Development Process

Ivar Jacobson, Grady Booch, and James Rumbaugh

Addison-Wesley Object Technology Series

The Unified Software Development Process goes beyond other object-oriented analysis and design methods by detailing a family of processes that incorporate the complete lifecycle of software development. This new book, representing the collaboration of Ivar Jacobson, Grady Booch, and James Rumbaugh, clearly describes the different higher-level constructs—notation as well as semantics—used in the models. Thus, stereotypes such as use cases and actors, packages, classes, interfaces, active classes, processes and threads, nodes, and most relations are described intuitively in the context of a model.

0-201-57169-2 • Hardcover • 512 pages • ©1999

The Rational Unified Process

An Introduction

Philippe Kruchten

Addison-Wesley Object Technology Series

This concise book offers a quick introduction to the concepts, structure, content, and motivation of the Rational Unified Process. This revolutionary software development process provides a disciplined approach to assigning, managing, and completing tasks within a software development organization, and is the first development process to exploit the full capabilities of the industry-standard Unified Modeling Language. *The Rational Unified Process* is unique in that it captures many of the proven best practices in modern software development and presents them in a form that can be tailored to a wide range of projects and organizations.

0-201-60459-0 • Paperback • 272 pages • ©1999

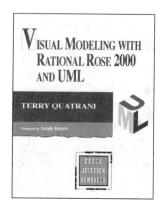

Visual Modeling with Rational Rose 2000 and UML

Terry Quatrani

Addison-Wesley Object Technology Series

Terry Quatrani, the Rose Evangelist from Rational Software Corporation, uses a simplified case study to teach readers how to analyze and design an application using UML and how to implement the application using Rational Rose 2000. With the practical direction offered in this updated book, you will be able to specify, visualize, document, and create software solutions. Highlights include examination of system behavior from a use case approach, a discussion of the concepts and notations used for finding objects and classes, an introduction to the notation needed to create and document a system's architecture, and a review of the iteration planning process.

0-201-69961-3 • Paperback • 240 pages • ©2000

Use Case Driven Object Modeling with UML

A Practical Approach
Doug Rosenberg, with Kendall Scott
Addison-Wesley Object Technology Series

This book presents a streamlined approach to UML modeling that includes a minimal but sufficient set of diagrams and techniques you can use to get from use cases to code quickly and efficiently. *Use Case Driven Object Modeling with UML* provides practical guidance that shows developers how to produce UML models with minimal startup time, while maintaining traceability from user requirements through detailed design and coding. The authors draw upon their extensive industry experience to present proven methods for driving the object modeling process forward from use cases in a simple and straightforward manner.

0-201-43289-7 • Paperback • 192 pages • ©1999

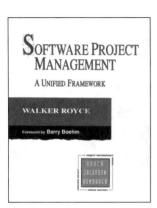

Software Project Management

A Unified Framework
Walker Royce
Addison-Wesley Object Technology Series

This book presents a new management framework uniquely suited to the complexities of modern software development. Walker Royce's pragmatic perspective exposes the shortcomings of many well-accepted management priorities and equips software professionals with state-of-the-art knowledge derived from his twenty years of successful from-the-trenches management experience. In short, the book provides the software industry with field-proven benchmarks for making tactical decisions and strategic choices that will enhance an organization's probability of success.

0-201-30958-0 • Hardcover • 448 pages • ©1998

The Unified Modeling Language Reference Manual

James Rumbaugh, Ivar Jacobson, and Grady Booch
Addison-Wesley Object Technology Series

James Rumbaugh, Ivar Jacobson, and Grady Booch have created the definitive reference to the UML. This two-color book covers every aspect and detail of the UML and presents the modeling language in a useful reference format that serious software architects or programmers should have on their bookshelf. The book is organized by topic and designed for quick access. The authors also provide the necessary information to enable existing OMT, Booch, and OOSE notation users to make the transition to UML. The book provides an overview of the semantic foundation of the UML through a concise appendix.

0-201-30998-X • Hardcover with CD-ROM • 576 pages • ©1999

Applying Use Cases
A Practical Guide
Geri Schneider and Jason P. Winters
Addison-Wesley Object Technology Series

Applying Use Cases provides a practical and clear introduction to developing use cases, demonstrating their use via a continuing case study. Using the Unified Software Development Process as a framework and the Unified Modeling Language as a notation, the authors step the reader through applying use cases in the different phases of the process, focusing on where and how use cases are best applied. The book also offers insight into the common mistakes and pitfalls that can plague an object-oriented project.

0-201-30981-5 • Paperback • 208 pages • ©1998

Enterprise Computing with Objects
From Client/Server Environments to the Internet
Yen-Ping Shan and Ralph H. Earle
Addison-Wesley Object Technology Series

This book helps you place rapidly evolving technologies—such as the Internet, the World Wide Web, distributed computing, object technology, and client/server systems—in their appropriate contexts when preparing for the development, deployment, and maintenance of information systems. The authors distinguish what is essential from what is incidental, while imparting a clear understanding of how the underlying technologies fit together. The book examines essential topics, including data persistence, security, performance, scalability, and development tools.

0-201-32566-7 • Paperback • 448 pages • ©1998

Addison-Wesley Computer and Engineering Publishing Group

How to Interact with Us

1. Visit our Web site

http://www.awl.com/cseng

When you think you've read enough, there's always more content for you at Addison-Wesley's web site. Our web site contains a directory of complete product information including:

- Chapters
- Exclusive author interviews
- Links to authors' pages
- Tables of contents
- Source code

You can also discover what tradeshows and conferences Addison-Wesley will be attending, read what others are saying about our titles, and find out where and when you can meet our authors and have them sign your book.

2. Subscribe to Our Email Mailing Lists

Subscribe to our electronic mailing lists and be the first to know when new books are publishing. Here's how it works: Sign up for our electronic mailing at **http://www.awl.com/cseng/mailinglists.html**. Just select the subject areas that interest you and you will receive notification via email when we publish a book in that area.

3. Contact Us via Email

cepubprof@awl.com
Ask general questions about our books.
Sign up for our electronic mailing lists.
Submit corrections for our web site.

bexpress@awl.com
Request an Addison-Wesley catalog.
Get answers to questions regarding your order or our products.

innovations@awl.com
Request a current Innovations Newsletter.

webmaster@awl.com
Send comments about our web site.

jcs@awl.com
Submit a book proposal.
Send errata for an Addison-Wesley book.

cepubpublicity@awl.com
Request a review copy for a member of the media interested in reviewing new Addison-Wesley titles.

We encourage you to patronize the many fine retailers who stock Addison-Wesley titles. Visit our online directory to find stores near you or visit our online store: **http://store.awl.com/** or call **800-824-7799**.

Addison Wesley Longman
Computer and Engineering Publishing Group
One Jacob Way, Reading, Massachusetts 01867 USA
TEL 781-944-3700 • FAX 781-942-3076

CD-ROM Warranty

Addison Wesley Longman, Inc. warrants the enclosed disc to be free of defects in materials and faulty workmanship under normal use for a period of ninety days after purchase. If a defect is discovered in the disc during this warranty period, a replacement disc can be obtained at no charge by sending the defective disc, postage prepaid, with proof of purchase to:

Editorial Department
Computer and Engineering Publishing Group
Addison-Wesley
One Jacob Way
Reading, Massachusetts 01867-3999

After the ninety-day period, a replacement disc will be sent upon receipt of the defective disc and a check or money order for $10.00, payable to Addison Wesley Longman, Inc.

Addison Wesley Longman, Inc. makes no warranty or representation, either expressed or implied, with respect to this software, its quality, performance, merchantability, or fitness for a particular purpose. In no event will Addison Wesley Longman, Inc., its distributors, or dealers be liable for direct, indirect, special, incidental, or consequential damages arising out of the use or inability to use the software. The exclusion of implied warranties is not permitted in some states. Therefore, the above exclusion may not apply to you. This warranty provides you with specific legal rights. There may be other rights that you may have that vary from state to state. The contents of this CD-ROM are intended for personal use only.

More information and updates are available at:

http://www.awl.com/cseng/titles/0-201-43313-3